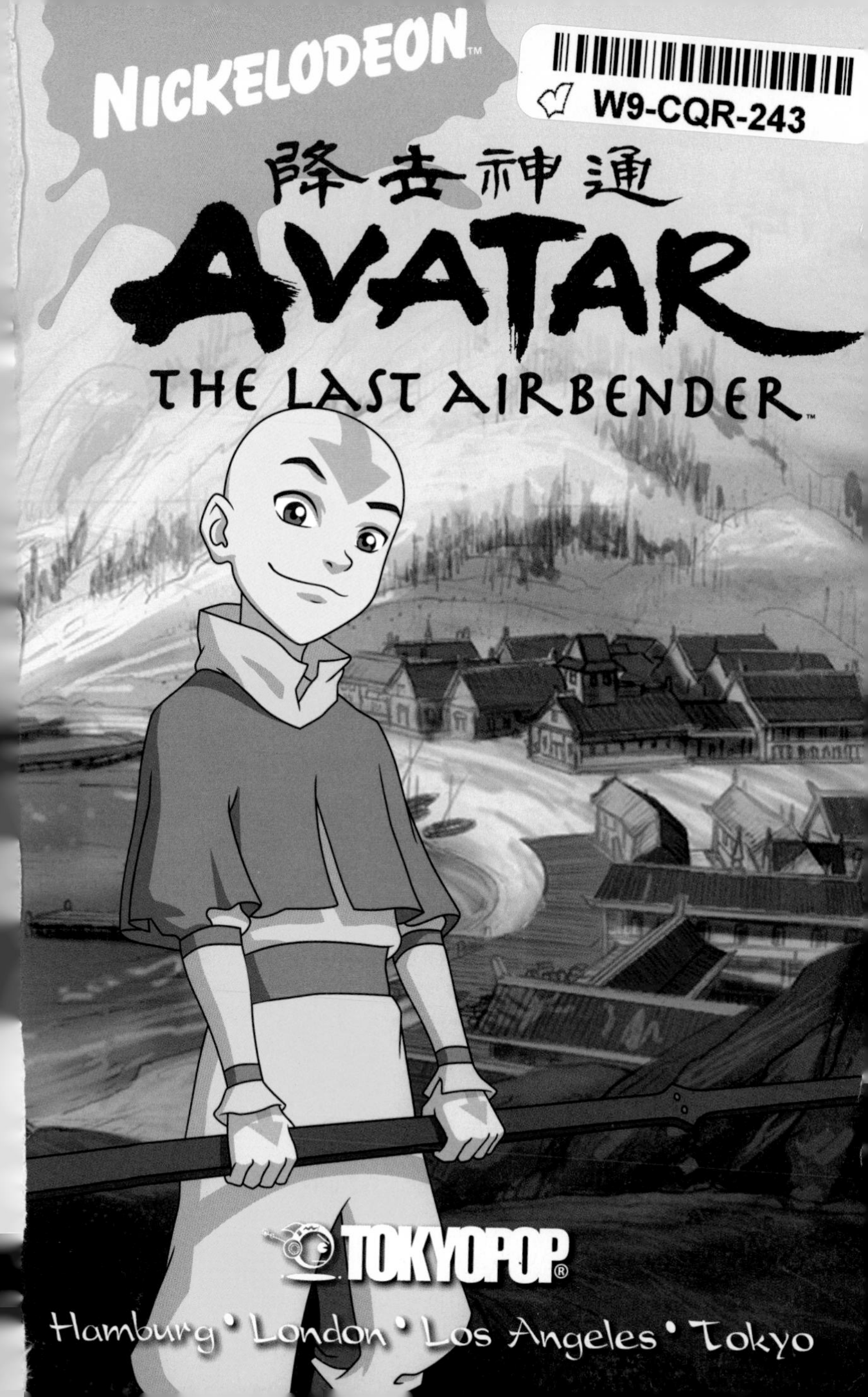

NICKELODEON™
W9-CQR-243
降世神通
AVATAR
THE LAST AIRBENDER™
TOKYOPOP®
Hamburg • London • Los Angeles • Tokyo

Contributing Editor - Robert Langhorn
Associate Editor - Katherine Schilling
Cover Designer - Monalisa J. de Asis
Graphic Designer, Letterer - Tomás Montalvo-Lagos

Digital Imaging Manager - Chris Buford
Production Managers - Elisabeth Brizzi
Senior Designer - Christian Lownds
Senior Editor - Julie Taylor
Managing Editor - Vy Nguyen
Editor in Chief - Rob Tokar
VP of Production - Ron Klamert
Publisher - Mike Kiley
President & C.O.O. - John Parker
C.E.O. & Chief Creative Officer - Stuart Levy

E-mail: info@TOKYOPOP.com
Come visit us online at www.TOKYOPOP.com

A **TOKYOPOP** Cine-Manga® Book
TOKYOPOP Inc.
5900 Wilshire Blvd., Suite 2000
Los Angeles, CA 90036

Avatar: The Last Airbender Chapter 4

ISBN: 978-1-59816-928-7

First TOKYOPOP® printing: February 2007

10 9 8 7 6 5 4 3

Printed in the USA

NICKELODEON™

降世神通

AVATAR

THE LAST AIRBENDER

Created By

Michael Dante DiMartino &

Bryan Konietzko

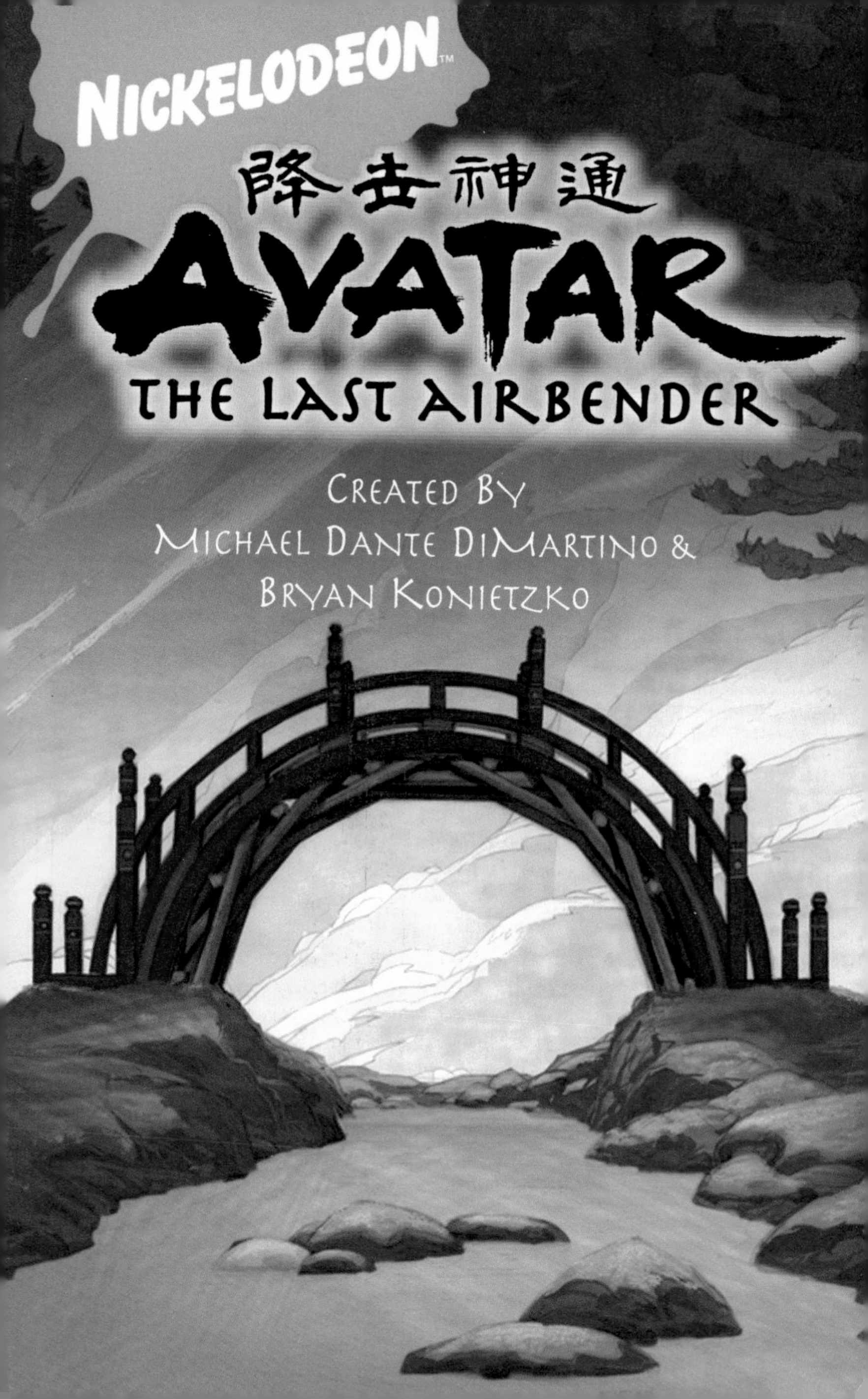

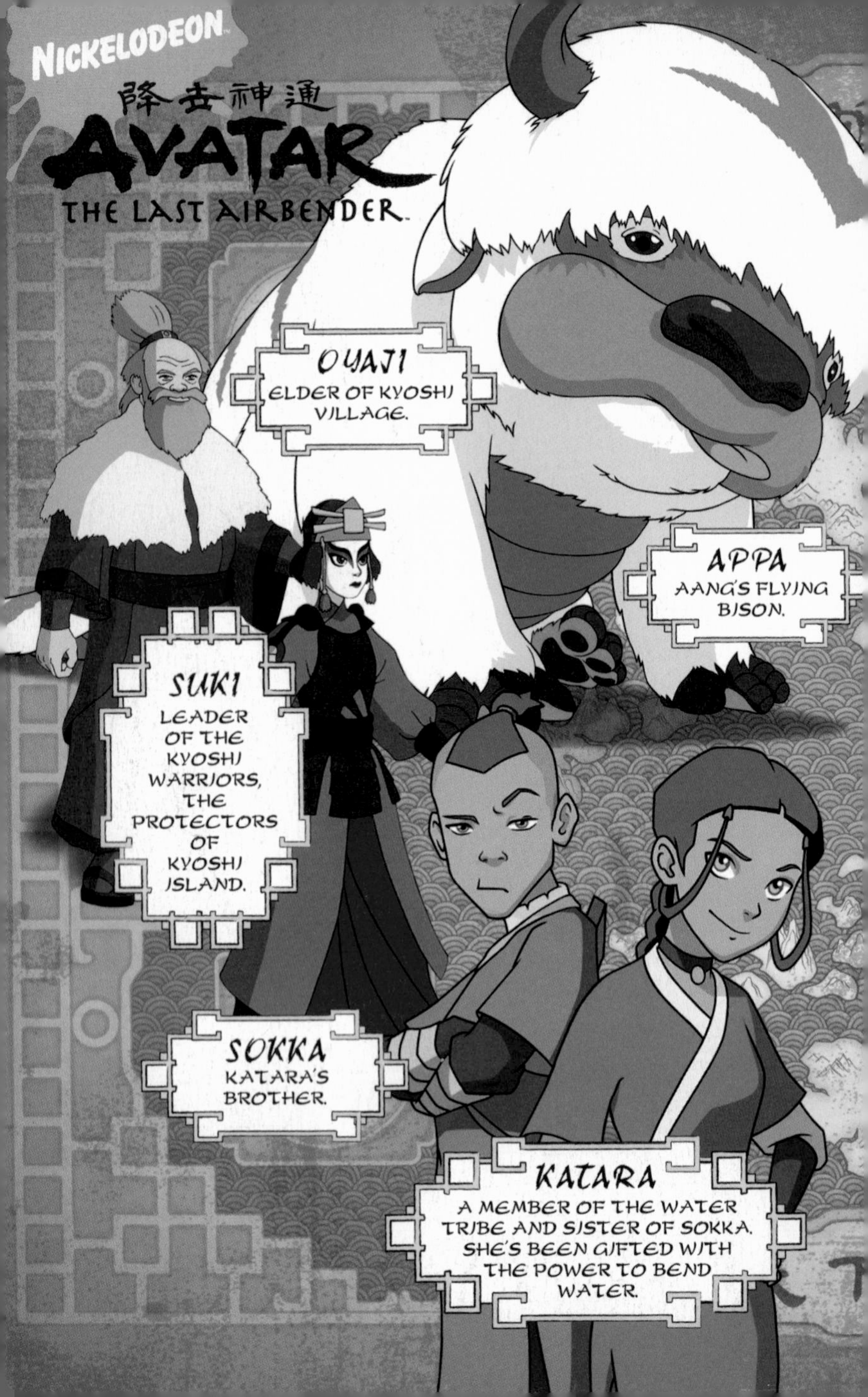
NICKELODEON
降世神通
AVATAR
THE LAST AIRBENDER
OYAJI
ELDER OF KYOSHI VILLAGE.
APPA
AANG'S FLYING BISON.
SUKI
LEADER OF THE KYOSHI WARRIORS, THE PROTECTORS OF KYOSHI ISLAND.
SOKKA
KATARA'S BROTHER.
KATARA
A MEMBER OF THE WATER TRIBE AND SISTER OF SOKKA. SHE'S BEEN GIFTED WITH THE POWER TO BEND WATER.

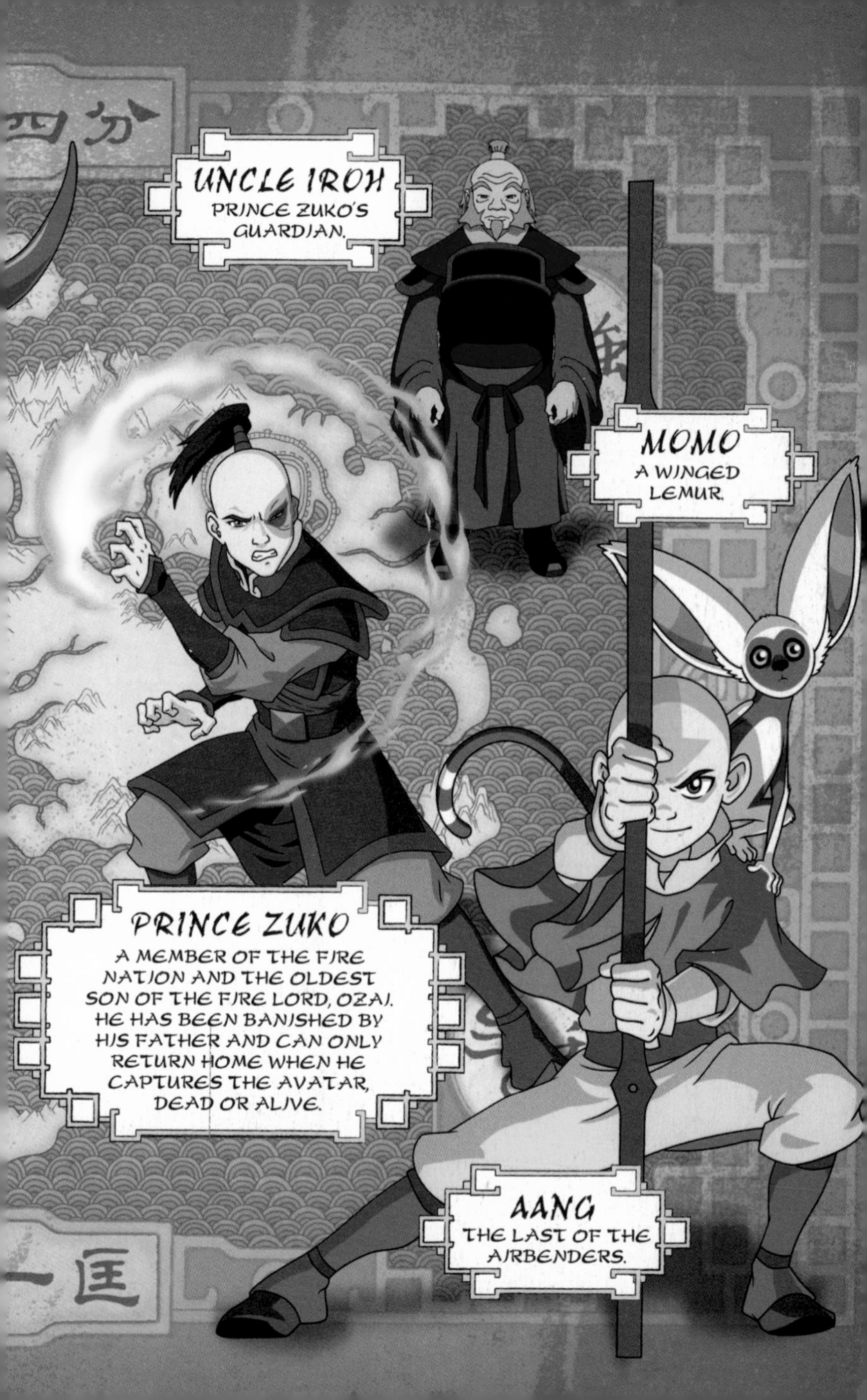

UNCLE IROH
PRINCE ZUKO'S GUARDIAN.
MOMO
A WINGED LEMUR.
PRINCE ZUKO
A MEMBER OF THE FIRE NATION AND THE OLDEST SON OF THE FIRE LORD, OZAI. HE HAS BEEN BANISHED BY HIS FATHER AND CAN ONLY RETURN HOME WHEN HE CAPTURES THE AVATAR, DEAD OR ALIVE.
AANG
THE LAST OF THE AIRBENDERS.

NICKELODEON™

降击神通

AVATAR

THE LAST AIRBENDER™

CHAPTER 4: CONTENTS

THE STORY SO FAR...

AANG, ALONG WITH HIS TRUSTED FRIENDS, KATARA AND SOKKA, STUMBLED UPON A STARTLING DISCOVERY AT THE DESERTED AIR TEMPLE...PROVING ONCE AND FOR ALL THAT AANG REALLY IS THE LAST OF THE AIRBENDERS. THE PAIN OF HAVING LOST ALL HE CARED ABOUT THREW AANG INTO A WHIRLWIND OF ANGER AND POWER, BUT ONLY KATARA'S SOOTHING VOICE BROUGHT HIM BACK TO HIS SENSES. NOW, HAVING LEARNED TO LEAVE THE PAST BEHIND AND MOVE ON, THE GANG CONTINUES THEIR LONG JOURNEY TO THE NORTHERN WATER TRIBE, WHERE AANG CAN FIND A WATER-BENDING MASTER TO TRAIN HIM ON HIS PATH TO BECOMING THE TRUE AVATAR.

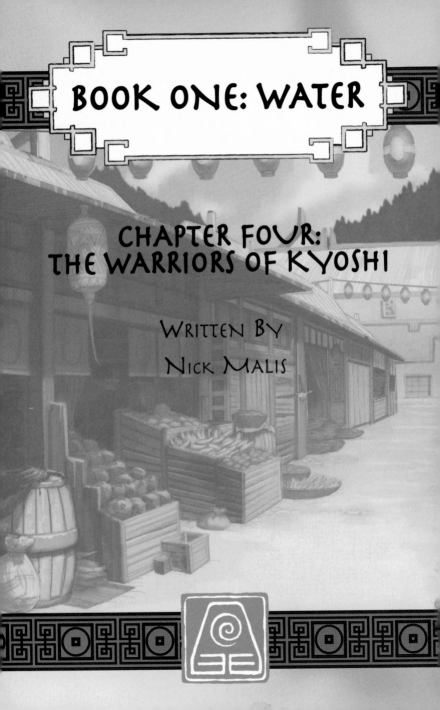

BOOK ONE: WATER

CHAPTER FOUR: THE WARRIORS OF KYOSHI

WRITTEN BY

NICK MALIS

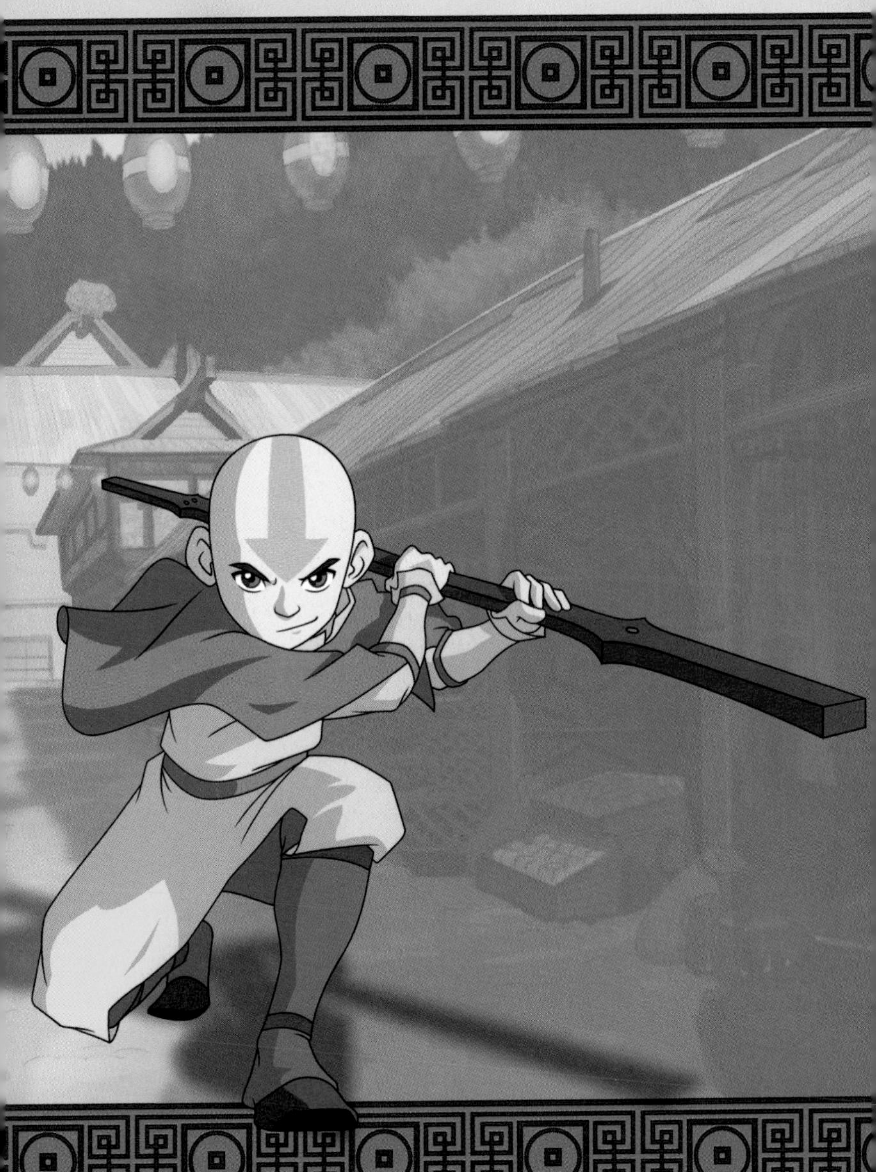

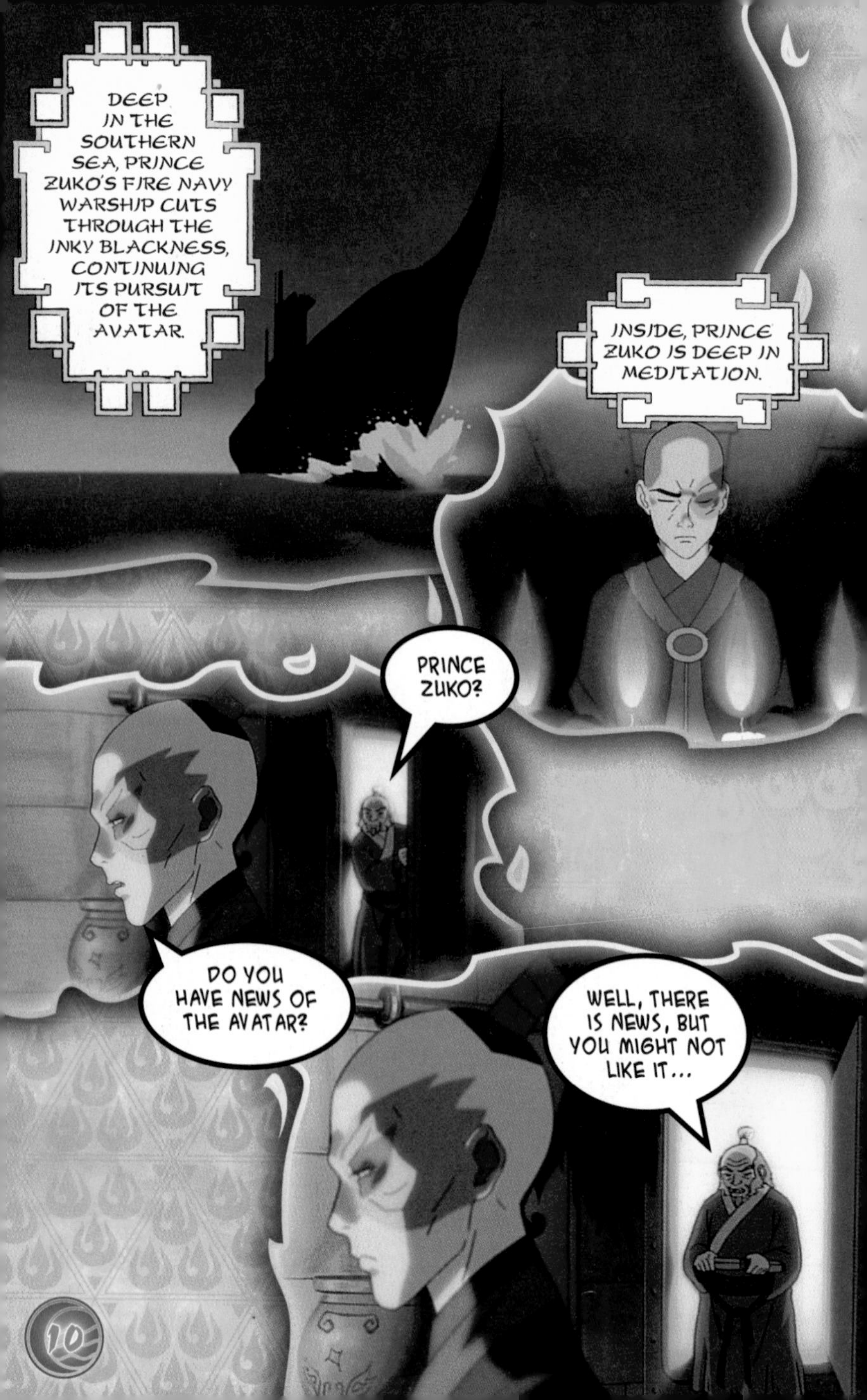
DEEP IN THE SOUTHERN SEA, PRINCE ZUKO'S FIRE NAVY WARSHIP CUTS THROUGH THE INKY BLACKNESS, CONTINUING ITS PURSUIT OF THE AVATAR.
INSIDE, PRINCE ZUKO IS DEEP IN MEDITATION.
PRINCE ZUKO?
DO YOU HAVE NEWS OF THE AVATAR?
WELL, THERE IS NEWS, BUT YOU MIGHT NOT LIKE IT...

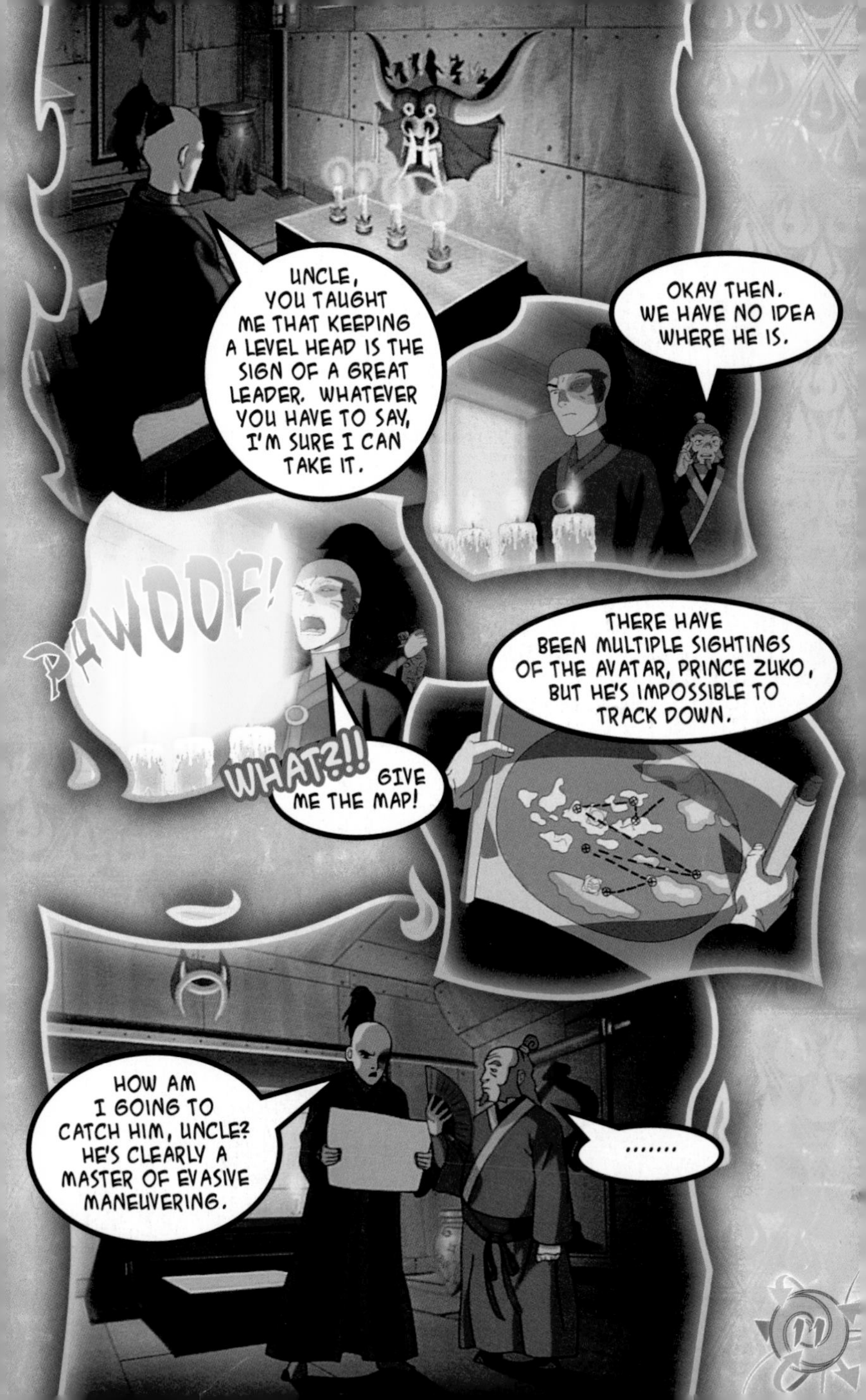
UNCLE, YOU TAUGHT ME THAT KEEPING A LEVEL HEAD IS THE SIGN OF A GREAT LEADER. WHATEVER YOU HAVE TO SAY, I'M SURE I CAN TAKE IT.
OKAY THEN. WE HAVE NO IDEA WHERE HE IS.
PAWOOF!
WHAT?!!
GIVE ME THE MAP!
THERE HAVE BEEN MULTIPLE SIGHTINGS OF THE AVATAR, PRINCE ZUKO, BUT HE'S IMPOSSIBLE TO TRACK DOWN.
HOW AM I GOING TO CATCH HIM, UNCLE? HE'S CLEARLY A MASTER OF EVASIVE MANEUVERING.
....

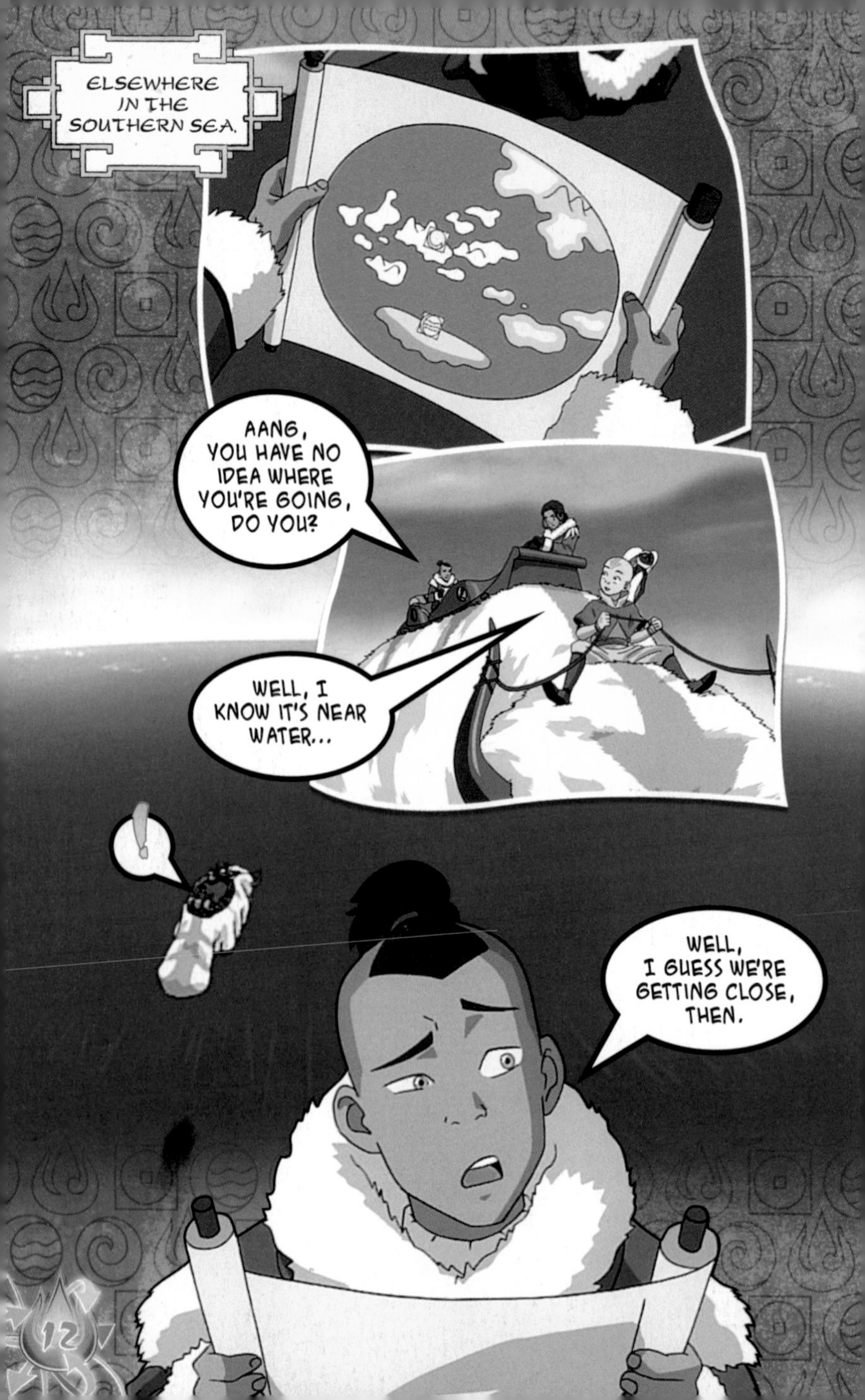

ELSEWHERE IN THE SOUTHERN SEA.
AANG, YOU HAVE NO IDEA WHERE YOU'RE GOING, DO YOU?
WELL, I KNOW IT'S NEAR WATER...
!
WELL, I GUESS WE'RE GETTING CLOSE, THEN.

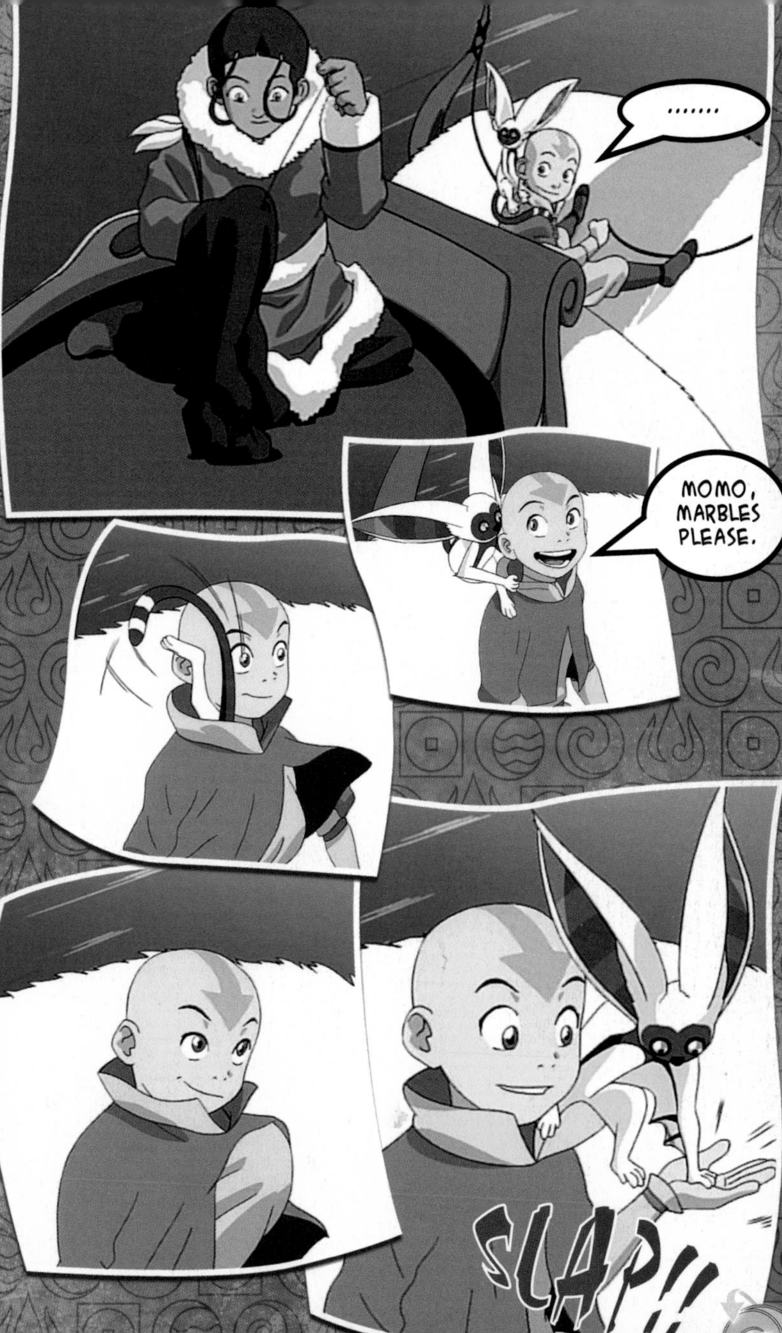
....
MOMO, MARBLES PLEASE.
SLAP!!

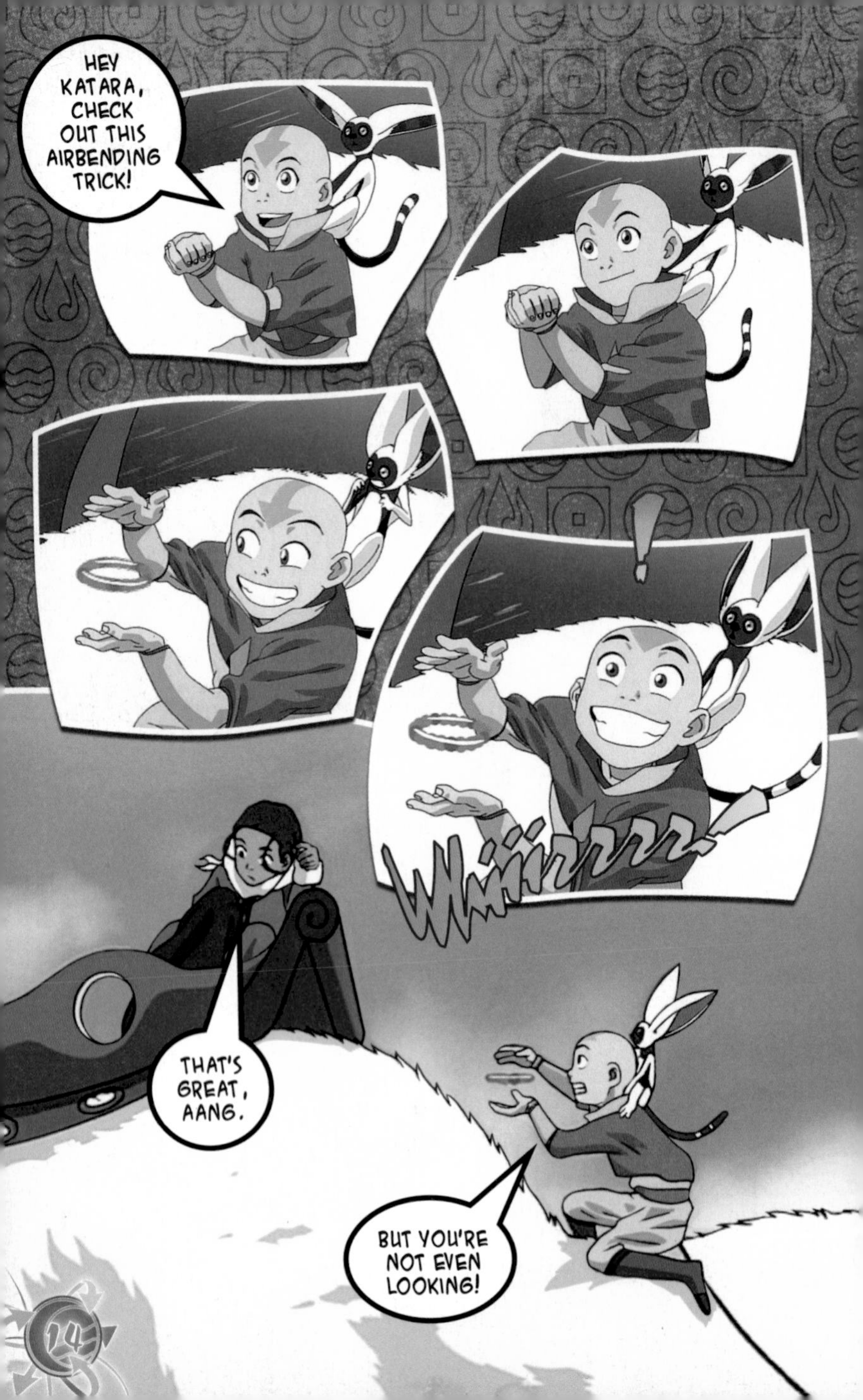
HEY KATARA, CHECK OUT THIS AIRBENDING TRICK!
!
Whirrrrr
THAT'S GREAT, AANG.
BUT YOU'RE NOT EVEN LOOKING!

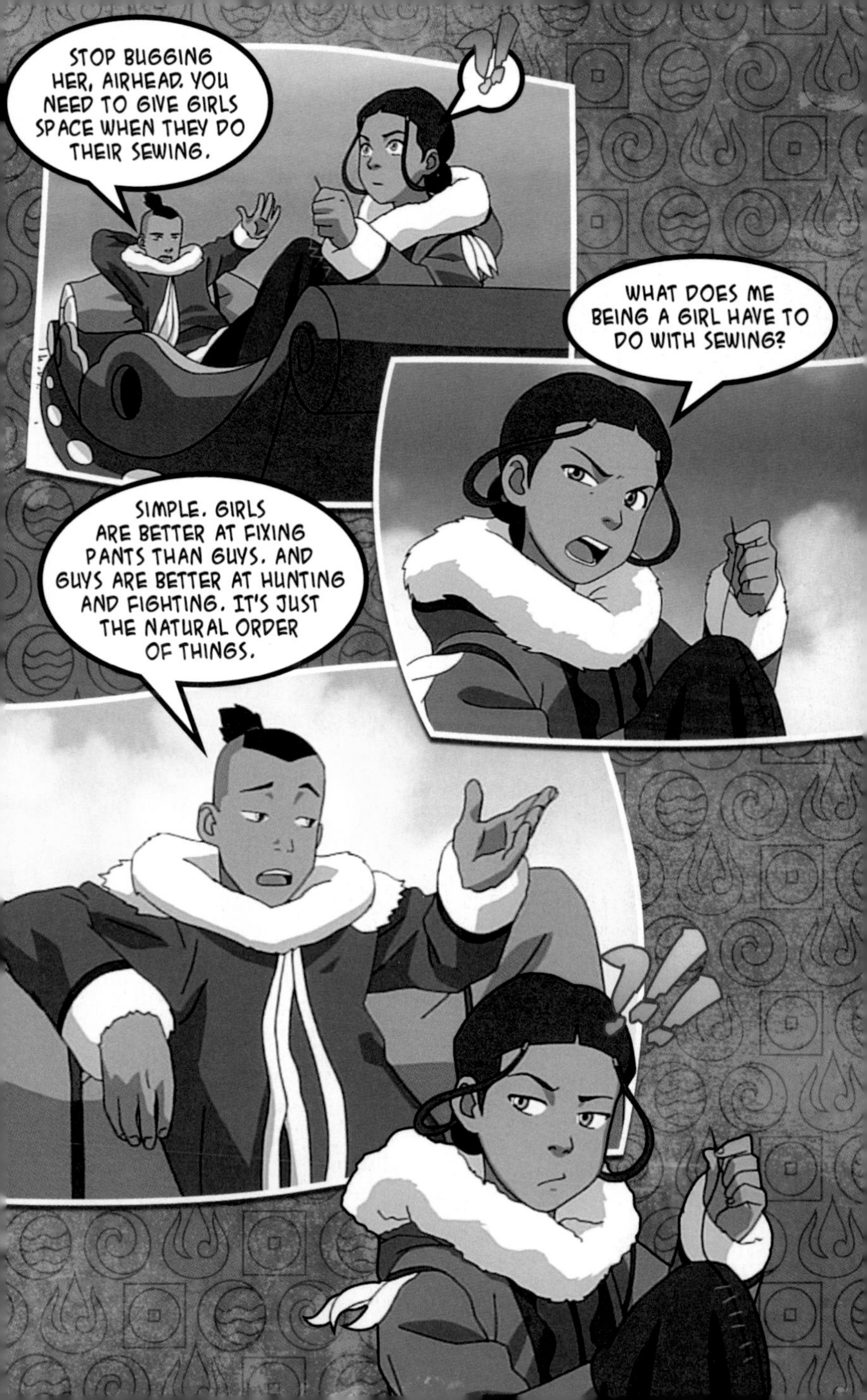
STOP BUGGING HER, AIRHEAD. YOU NEED TO GIVE GIRLS SPACE WHEN THEY DO THEIR SEWING.
WHAT DOES ME BEING A GIRL HAVE TO DO WITH SEWING?
SIMPLE. GIRLS ARE BETTER AT FIXING PANTS THAN GUYS. AND GUYS ARE BETTER AT HUNTING AND FIGHTING. IT'S JUST THE NATURAL ORDER OF THINGS.

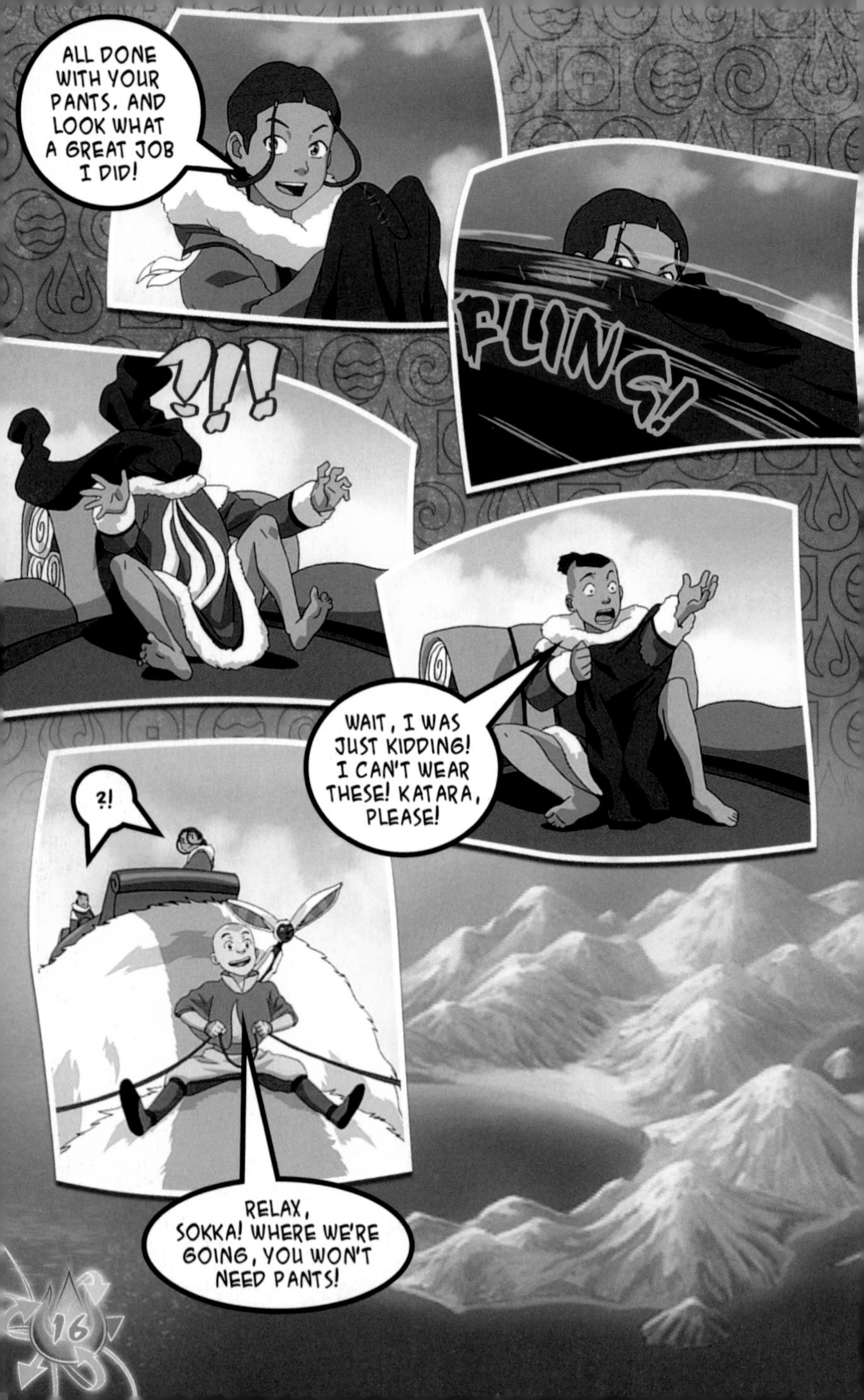
ALL DONE WITH YOUR PANTS. AND LOOK WHAT A GREAT JOB I DID!
FLING!
!!!
WAIT, I WAS JUST KIDDING! I CAN'T WEAR THESE! KATARA, PLEASE!
?!
RELAX, SOKKA! WHERE WE'RE GOING, YOU WON'T NEED PANTS!

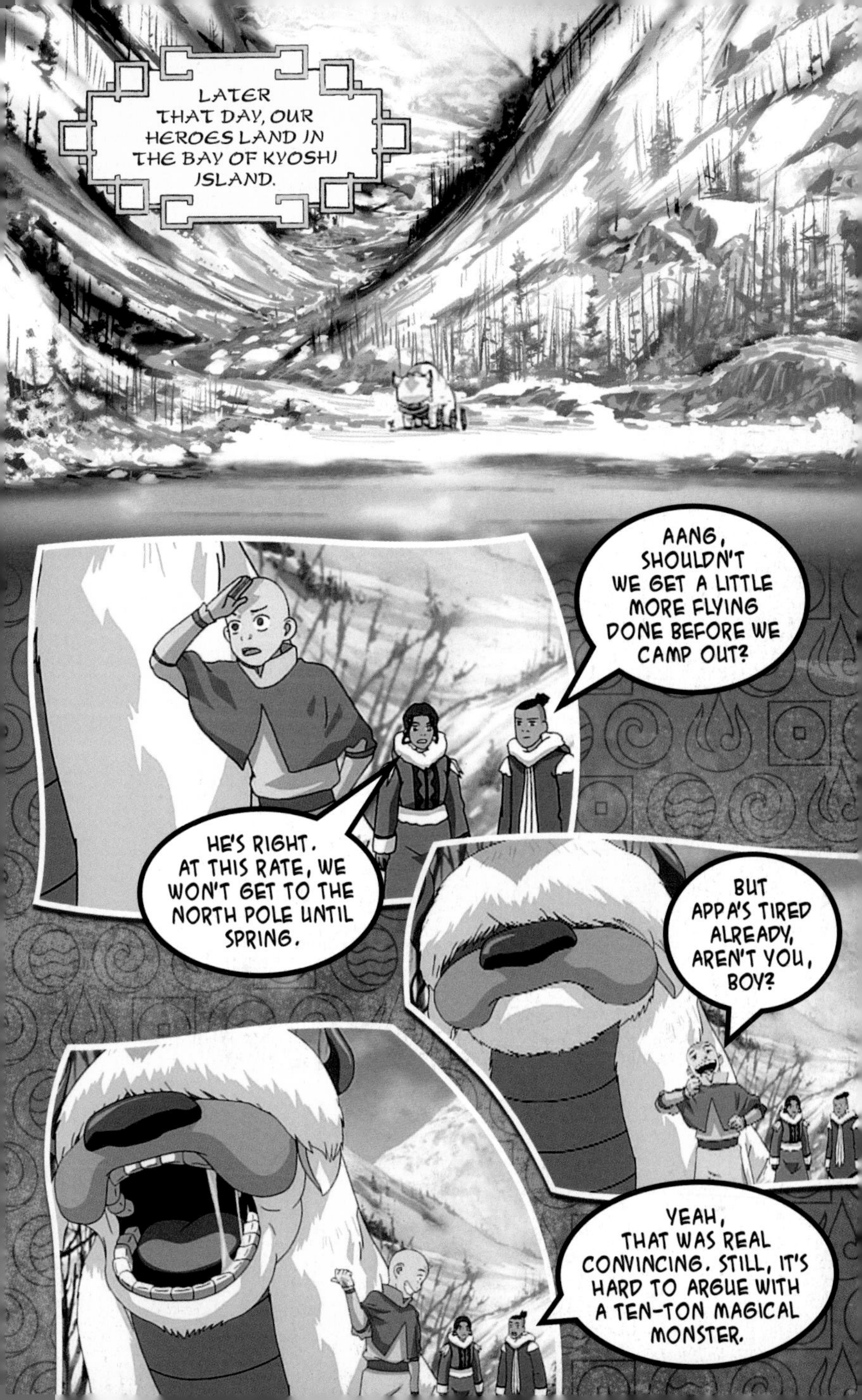
LATER THAT DAY, OUR HEROES LAND IN THE BAY OF KYOSHI ISLAND.
AANG, SHOULDN'T WE GET A LITTLE MORE FLYING DONE BEFORE WE CAMP OUT?
HE'S RIGHT. AT THIS RATE, WE WON'T GET TO THE NORTH POLE UNTIL SPRING.
BUT APPA'S TIRED ALREADY, AREN'T YOU, BOY?
YEAH, THAT WAS REAL CONVINCING. STILL, IT'S HARD TO ARGUE WITH A TEN-TON MAGICAL MONSTER.

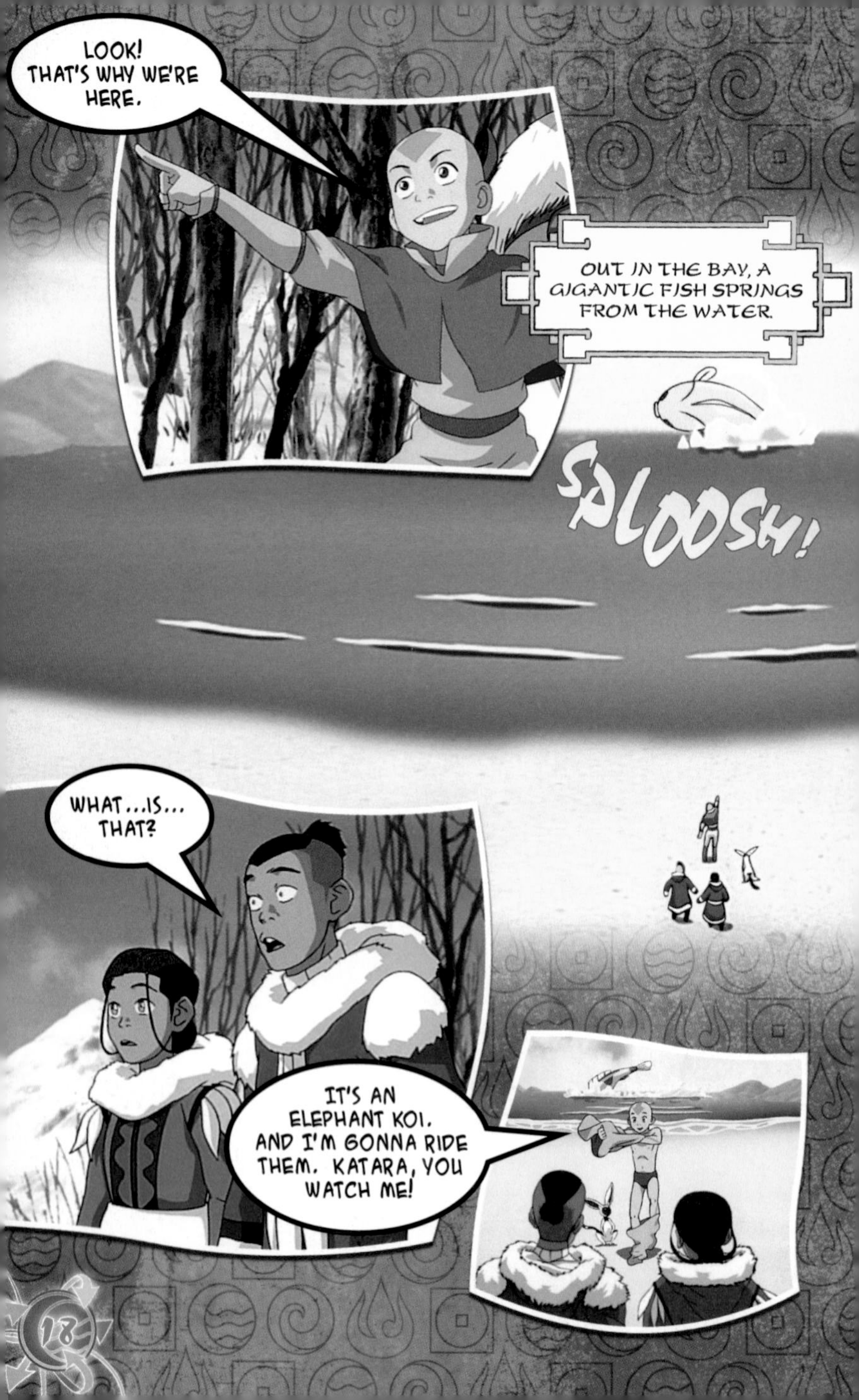
LOOK! THAT'S WHY WE'RE HERE.
OUT IN THE BAY, A GIGANTIC FISH SPRINGS FROM THE WATER.
SPLOOSH!
WHAT...IS... THAT?
IT'S AN ELEPHANT KOI. AND I'M GONNA RIDE THEM. KATARA, YOU WATCH ME!

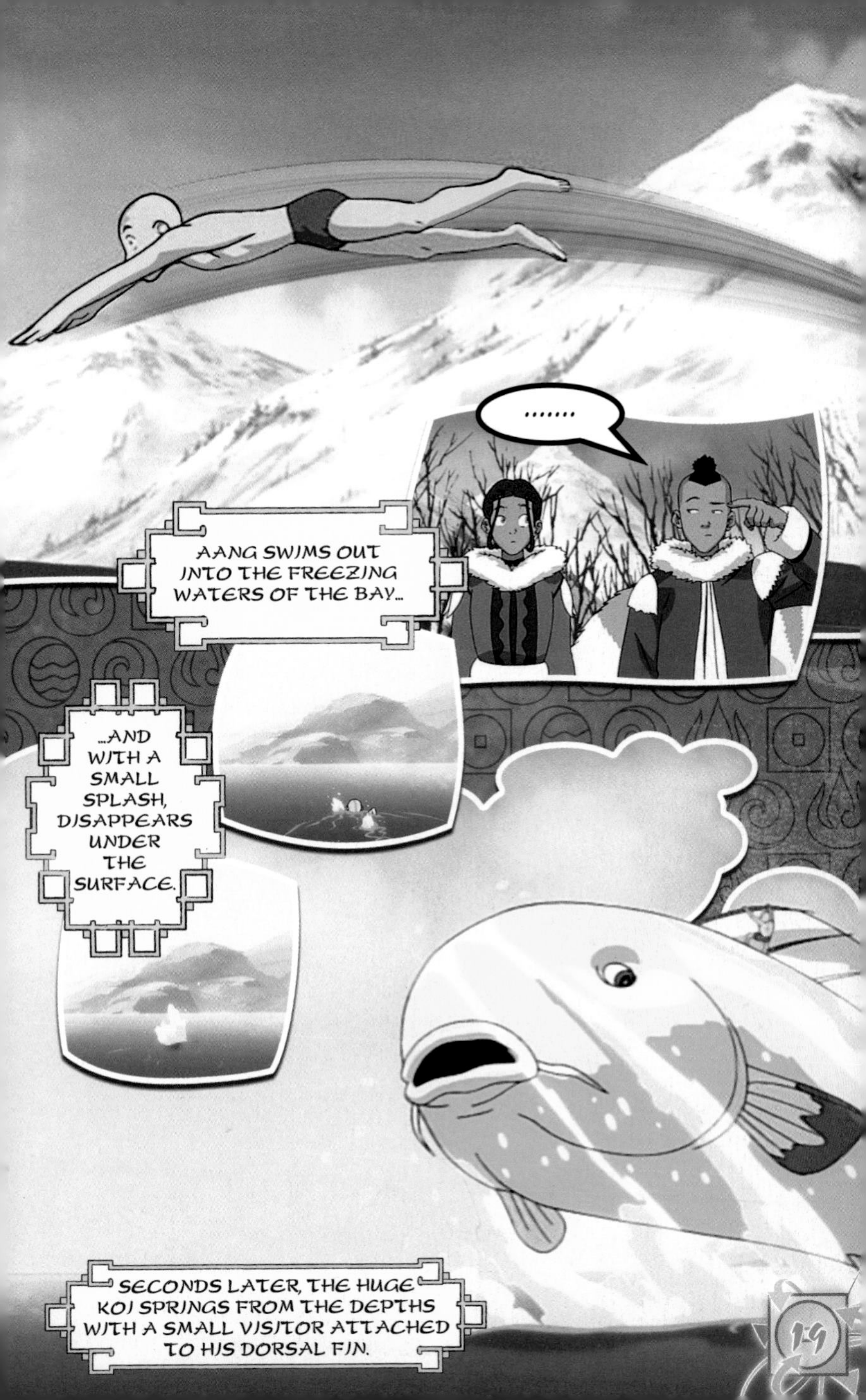
....
AANG SWIMS OUT INTO THE FREEZING WATERS OF THE BAY...
...AND WITH A SMALL SPLASH, DISAPPEARS UNDER THE SURFACE.
SECONDS LATER, THE HUGE KOI SPRINGS FROM THE DEPTHS WITH A SMALL VISITOR ATTACHED TO HIS DORSAL FIN.

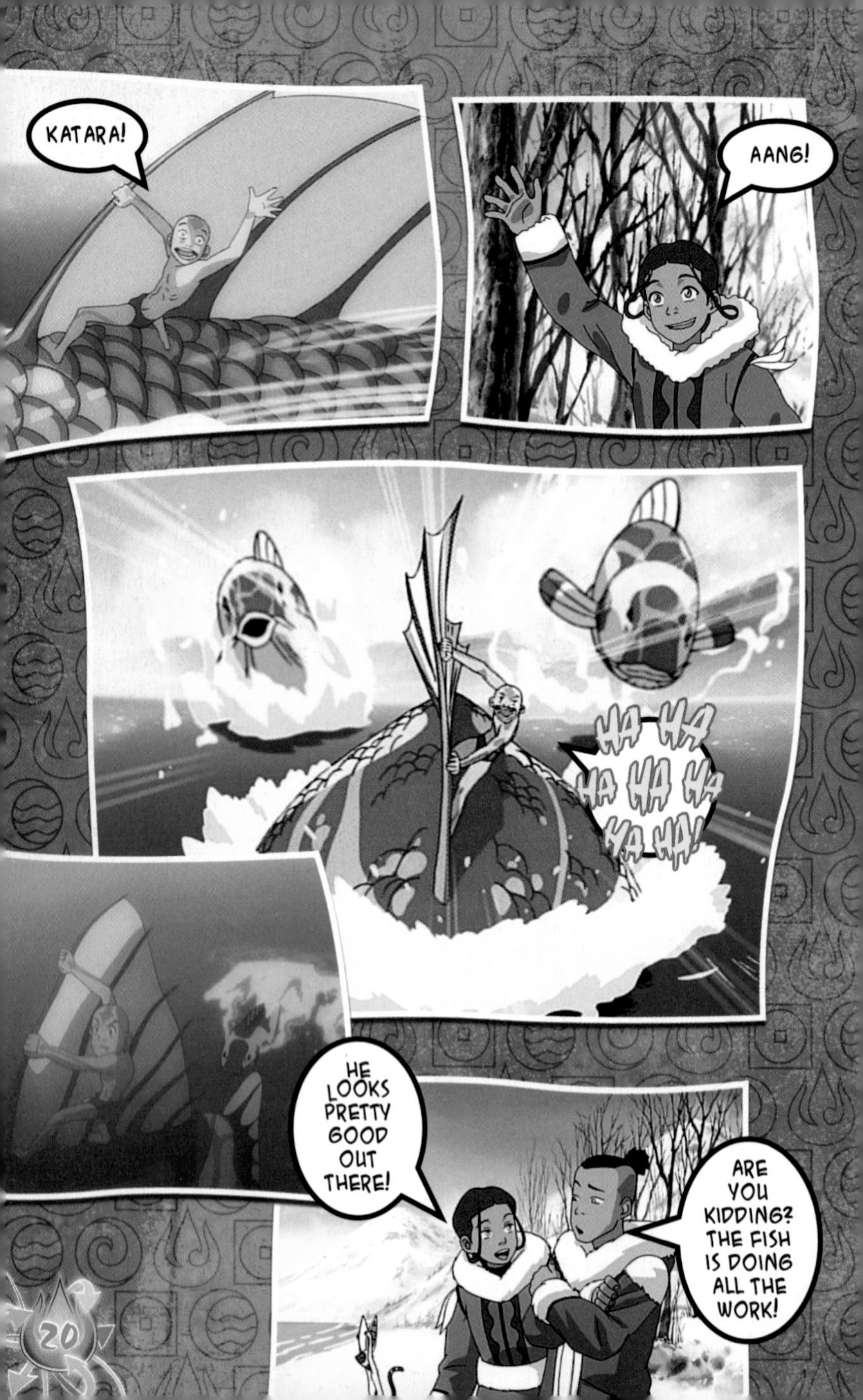
KATARA!
AANG!
HA HA HA HA HA HA HA!
HE LOOKS PRETTY GOOD OUT THERE!
ARE YOU KIDDING? THE FISH IS DOING ALL THE WORK!
20

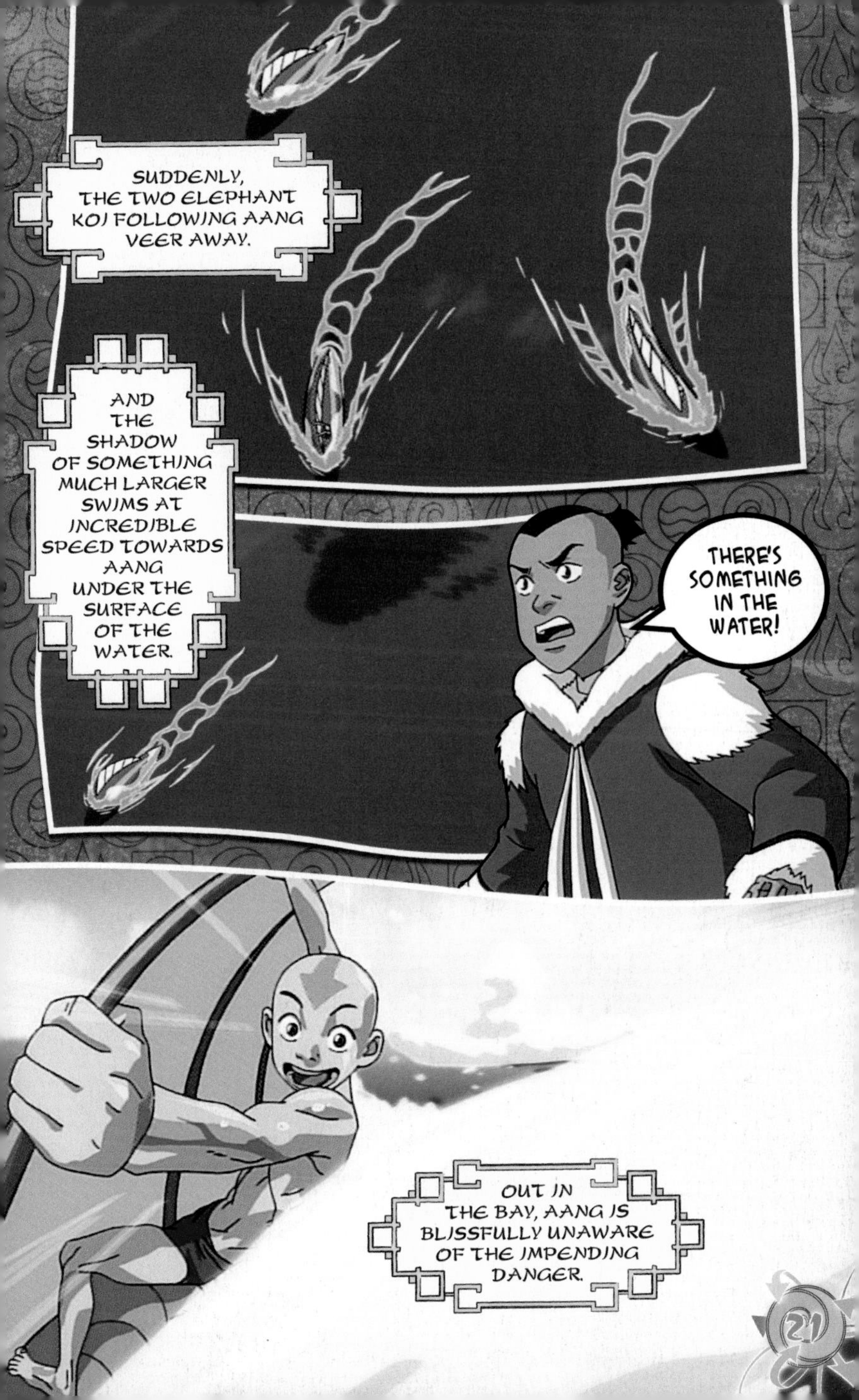
SUDDENLY, THE TWO ELEPHANT KOI FOLLOWING AANG VEER AWAY.
AND THE SHADOW OF SOMETHING MUCH LARGER SWIMS AT INCREDIBLE SPEED TOWARDS AANG UNDER THE SURFACE OF THE WATER.
THERE'S SOMETHING IN THE WATER!
OUT IN THE BAY, AANG IS BLISSFULLY UNAWARE OF THE IMPENDING DANGER.

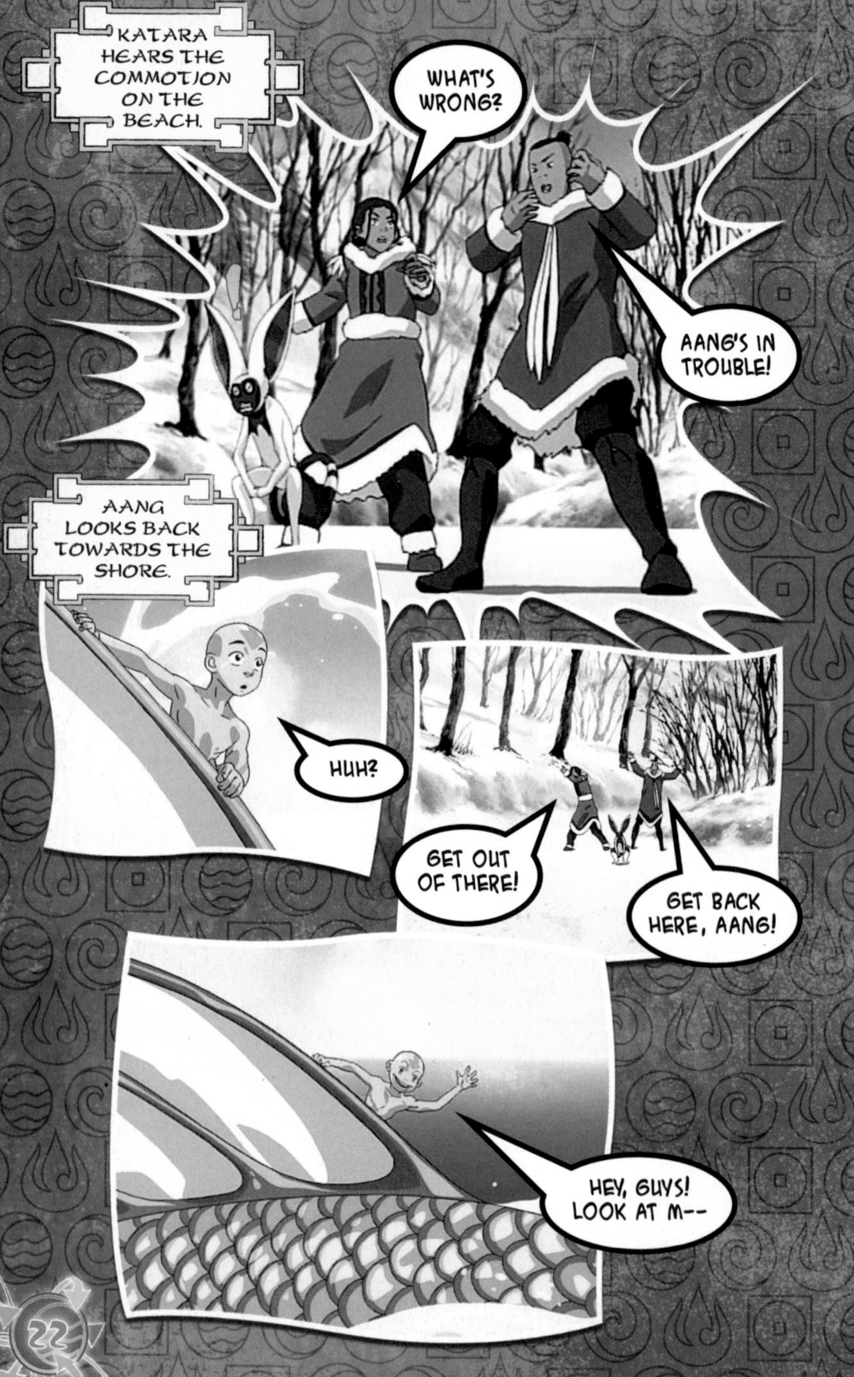
KATARA HEARS THE COMMOTION ON THE BEACH.
WHAT'S WRONG?
AANG'S IN TROUBLE!
AANG LOOKS BACK TOWARDS THE SHORE.
HUH?
GET OUT OF THERE!
GET BACK HERE, AANG!
HEY, GUYS! LOOK AT M--

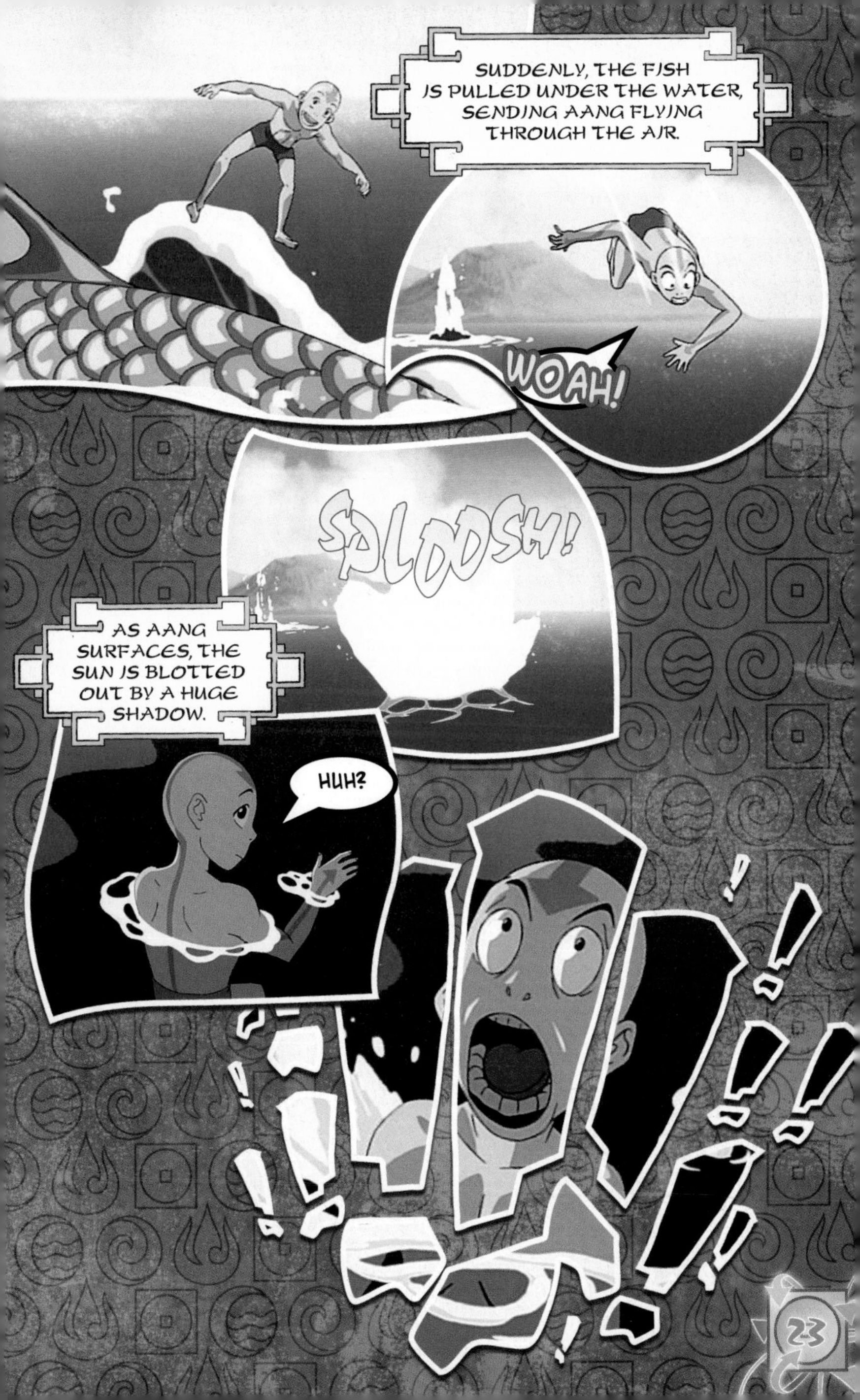
SUDDENLY, THE FISH IS PULLED UNDER THE WATER, SENDING AANG FLYING THROUGH THE AIR.
WOAH!
SPLOOSH!
AS AANG SURFACES, THE SUN IS BLOTTED OUT BY A HUGE SHADOW.
HUH?

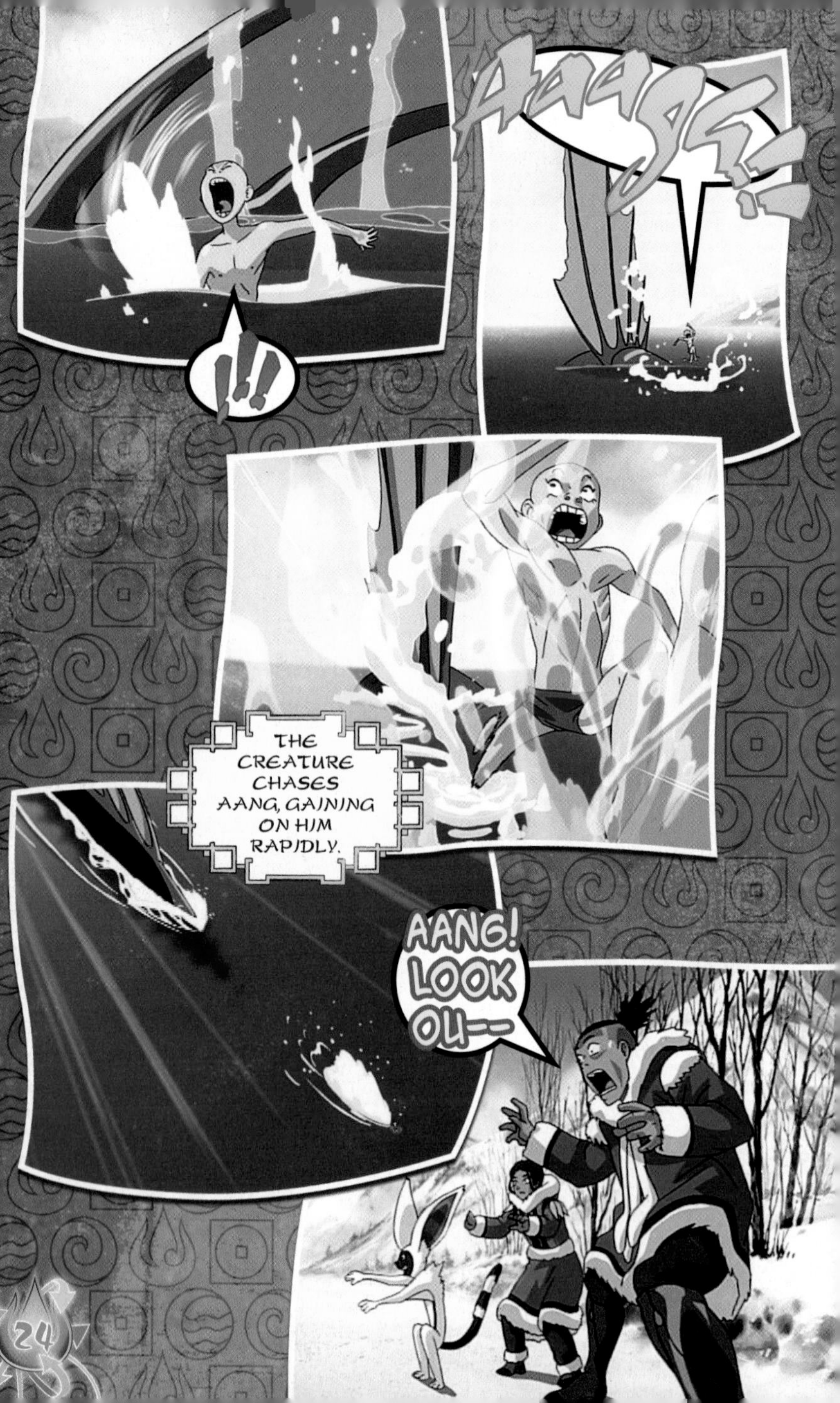
!!
AAAGH!!
THE CREATURE CHASES AANG, GAINING ON HIM RAPIDLY.
AANG! LOOK OU--

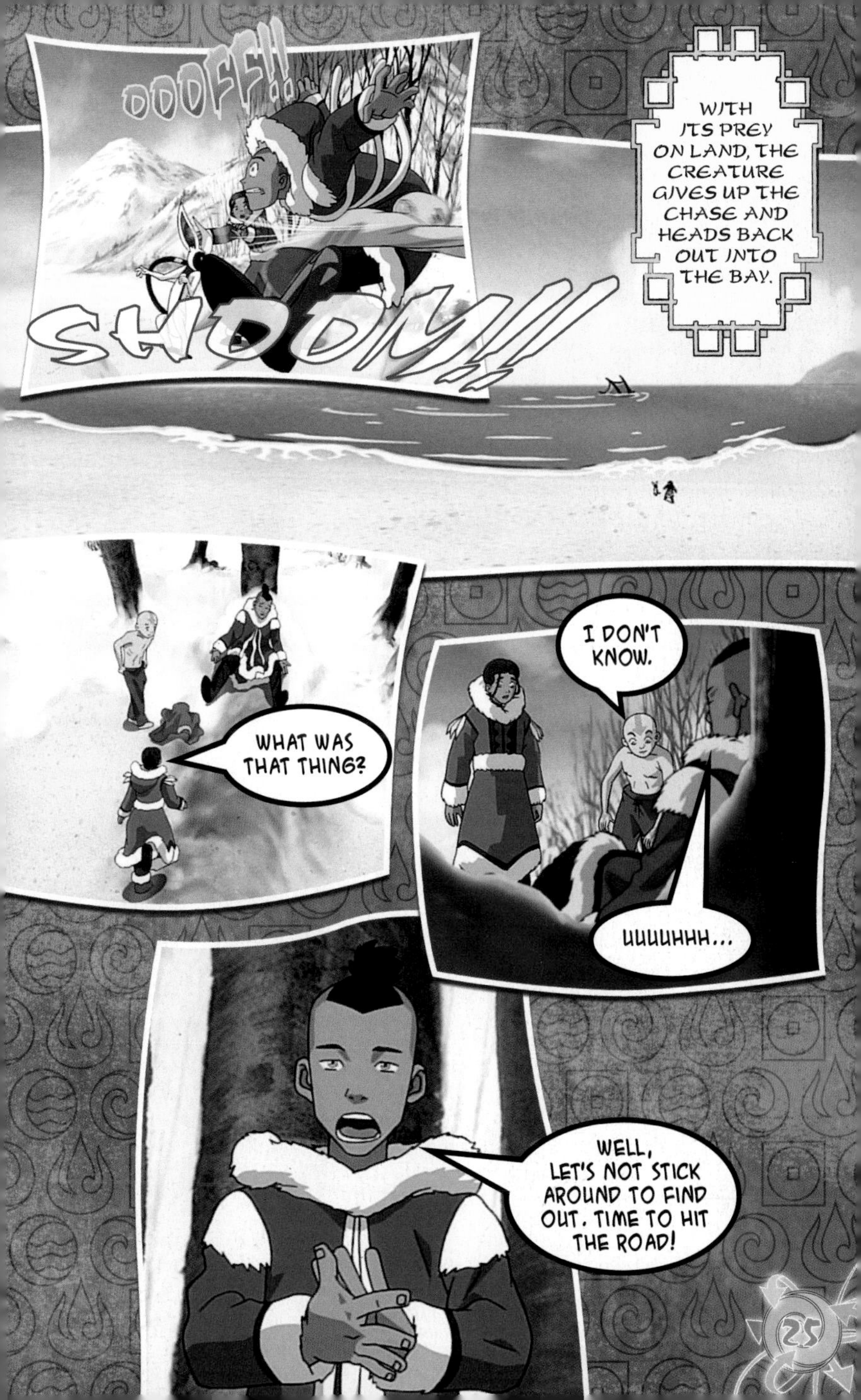
OOOFF!!
SHOOM!!
WITH ITS PREY ON LAND, THE CREATURE GIVES UP THE CHASE AND HEADS BACK OUT INTO THE BAY.
WHAT WAS THAT THING?
I DON'T KNOW.
UUUUHHH...
WELL, LET'S NOT STICK AROUND TO FIND OUT. TIME TO HIT THE ROAD!
25

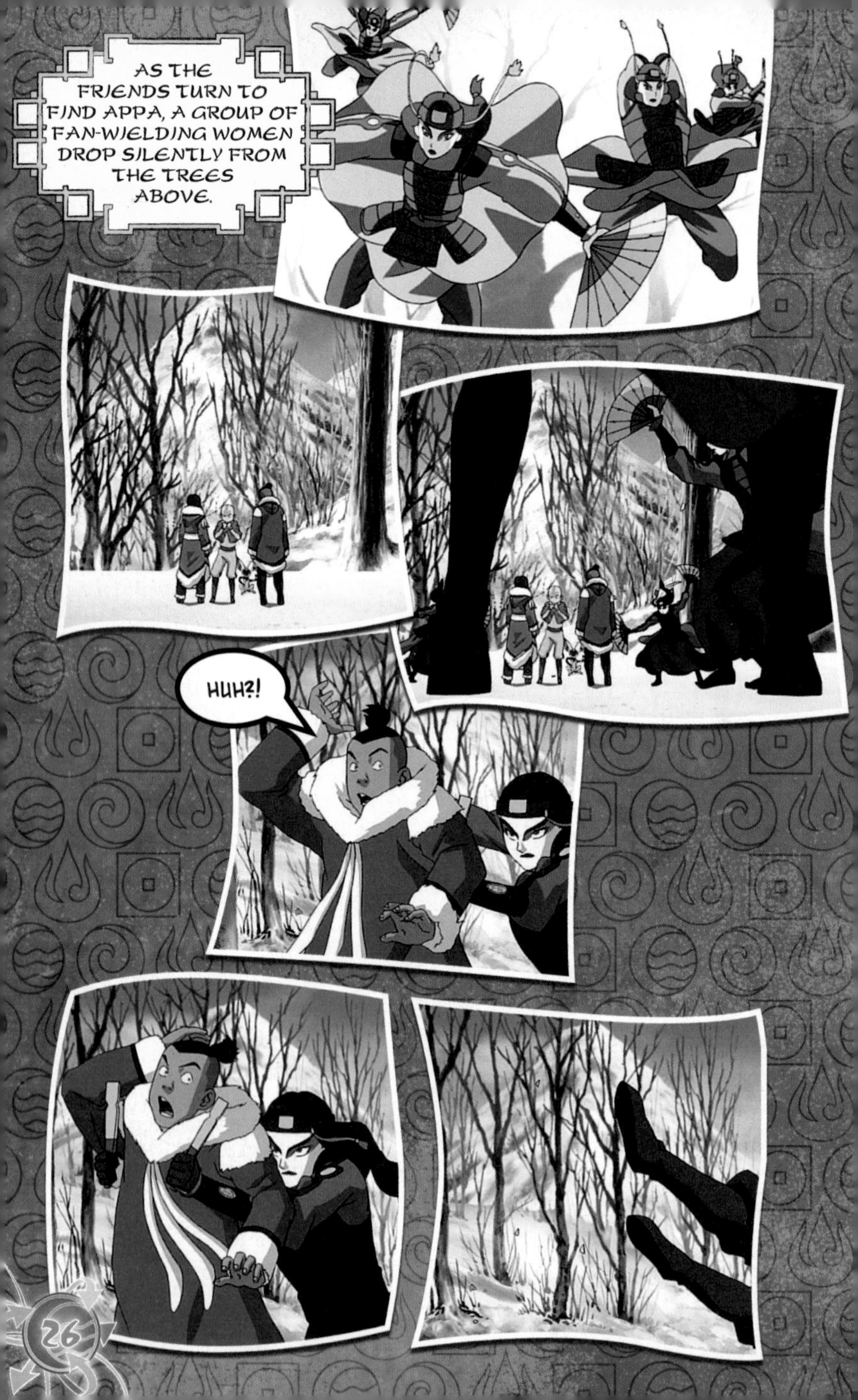
AS THE FRIENDS TURN TO FIND APPA, A GROUP OF FAN-WIELDING WOMEN DROP SILENTLY FROM THE TREES ABOVE.
HUH?!

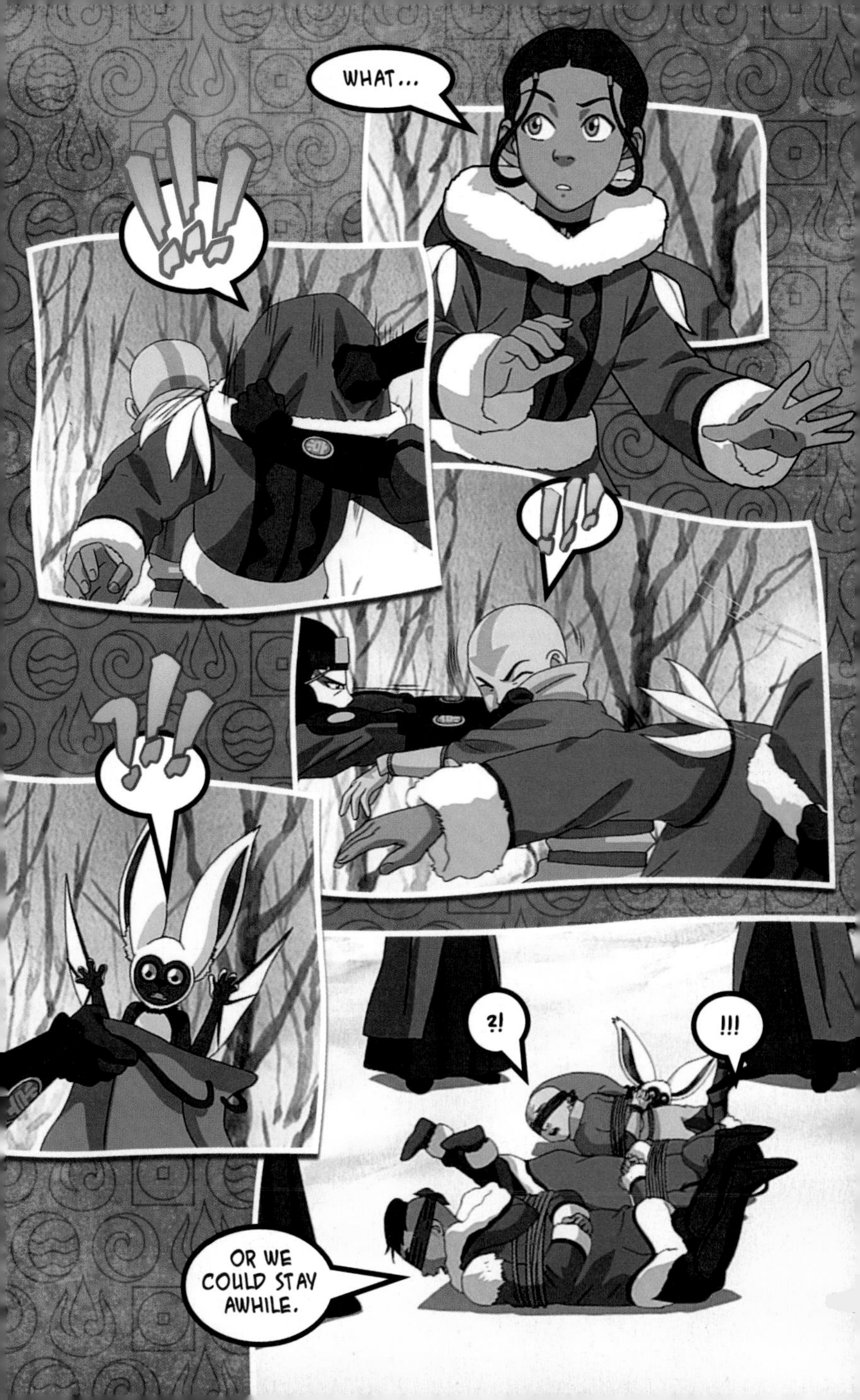
WHAT...
?!
!!!
OR WE COULD STAY AWHILE.

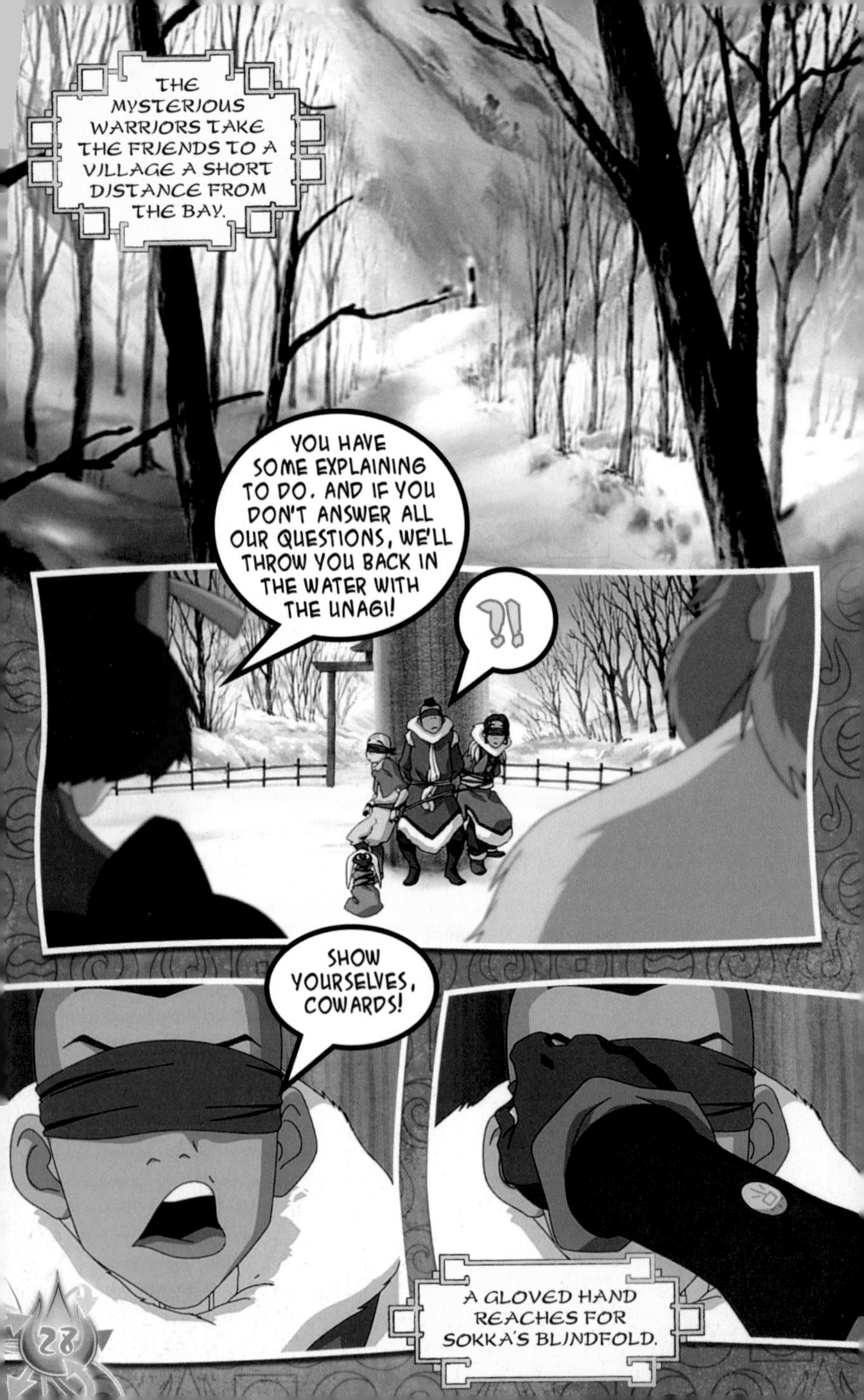
THE MYSTERIOUS WARRIORS TAKE THE FRIENDS TO A VILLAGE A SHORT DISTANCE FROM THE BAY.
YOU HAVE SOME EXPLAINING TO DO. AND IF YOU DON'T ANSWER ALL OUR QUESTIONS, WE'LL THROW YOU BACK IN THE WATER WITH THE UNAGI!
?!
SHOW YOURSELVES, COWARDS!
A GLOVED HAND REACHES FOR SOKKA'S BLINDFOLD.

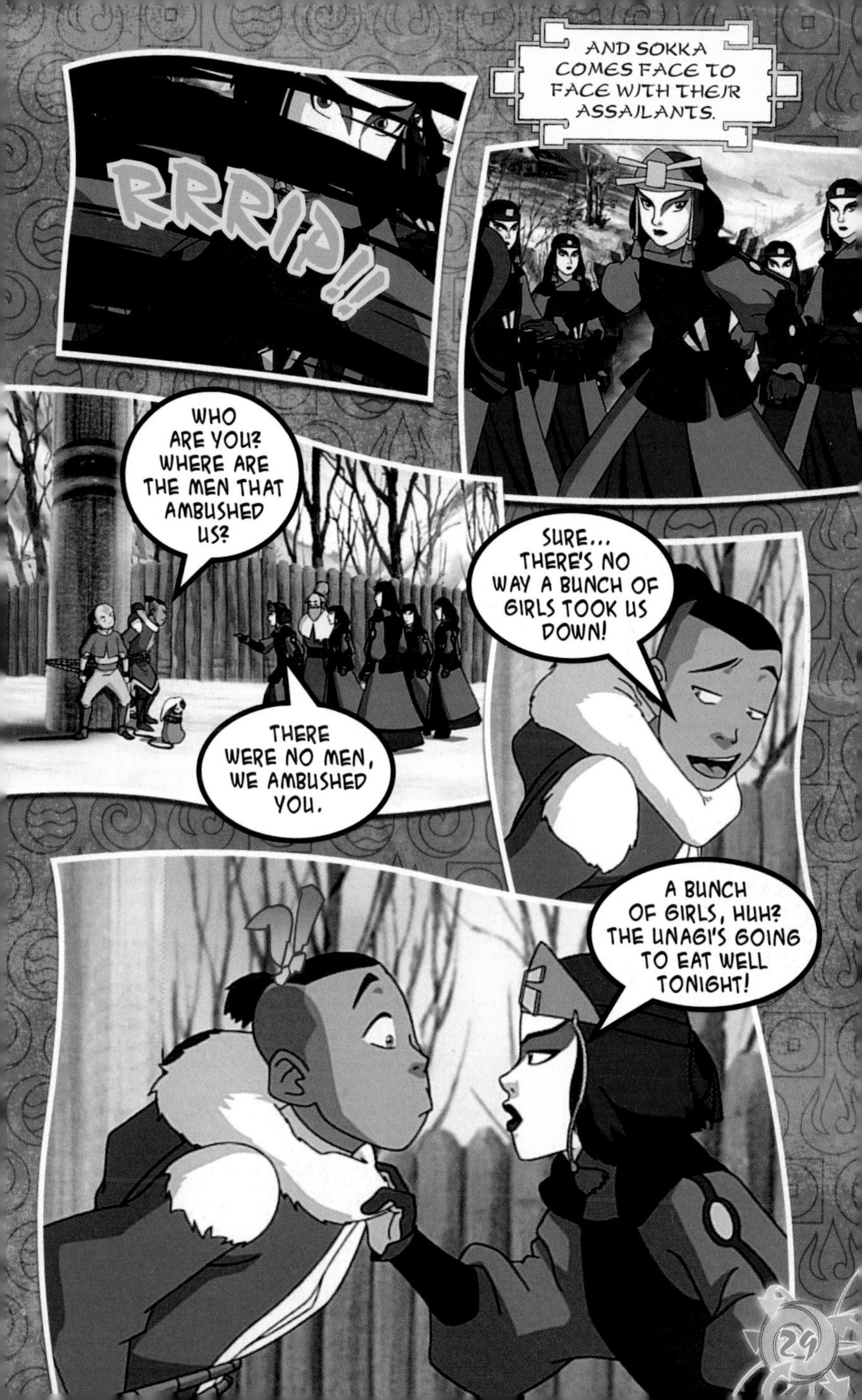

AND SOKKA COMES FACE TO FACE WITH THEIR ASSAILANTS.
RRRIP!!!
WHO ARE YOU? WHERE ARE THE MEN THAT AMBUSHED US?
THERE WERE NO MEN, WE AMBUSHED YOU.
SURE... THERE'S NO WAY A BUNCH OF GIRLS TOOK US DOWN!
A BUNCH OF GIRLS, HUH? THE UNAGI'S GOING TO EAT WELL TONIGHT!

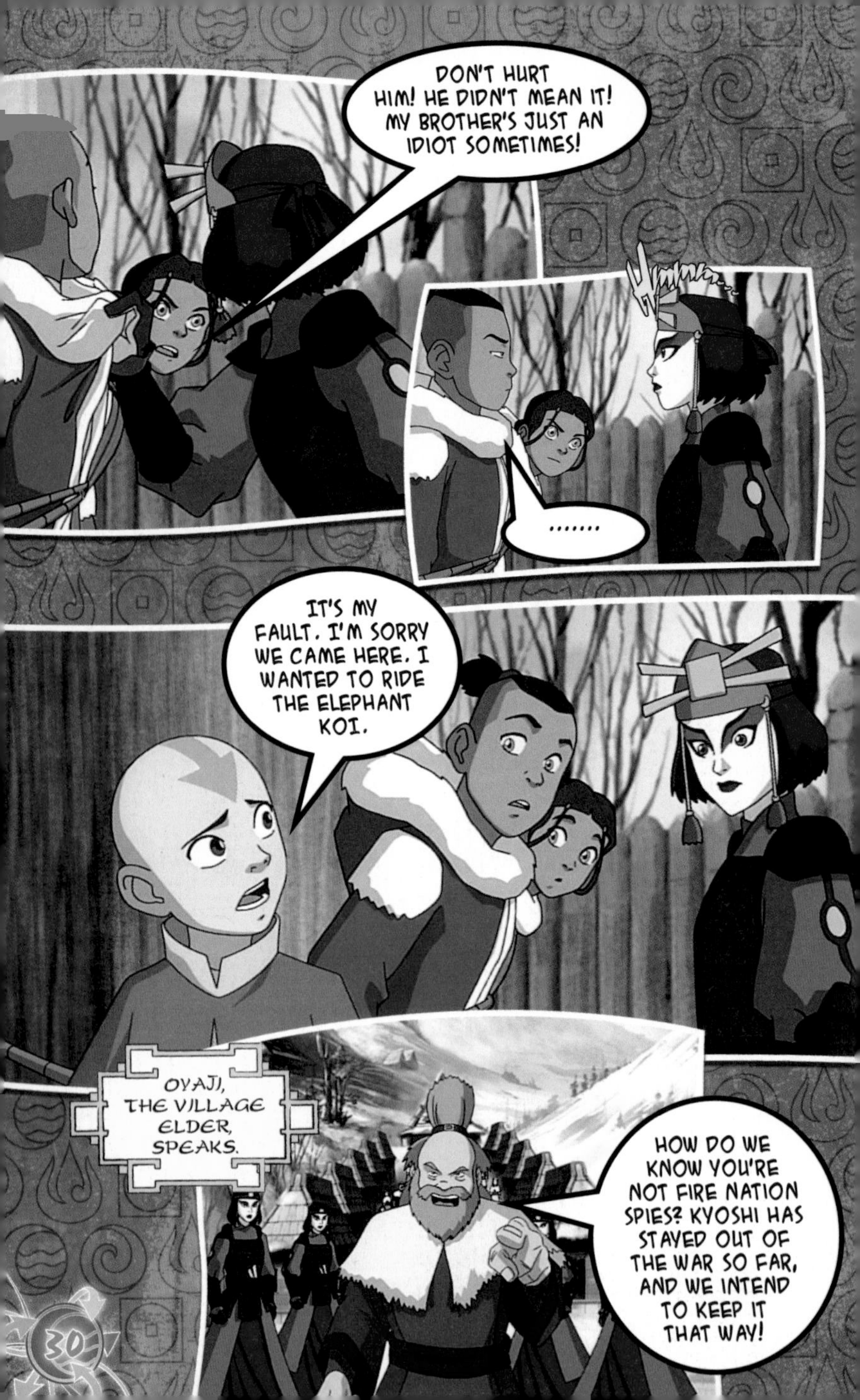
DON'T HURT HIM! HE DIDN'T MEAN IT! MY BROTHER'S JUST AN IDIOT SOMETIMES!
Hmmm...
....
IT'S MY FAULT. I'M SORRY WE CAME HERE. I WANTED TO RIDE THE ELEPHANT KOI.
OYAJI, THE VILLAGE ELDER, SPEAKS.
HOW DO WE KNOW YOU'RE NOT FIRE NATION SPIES? KYOSHI HAS STAYED OUT OF THE WAR SO FAR, AND WE INTEND TO KEEP IT THAT WAY!

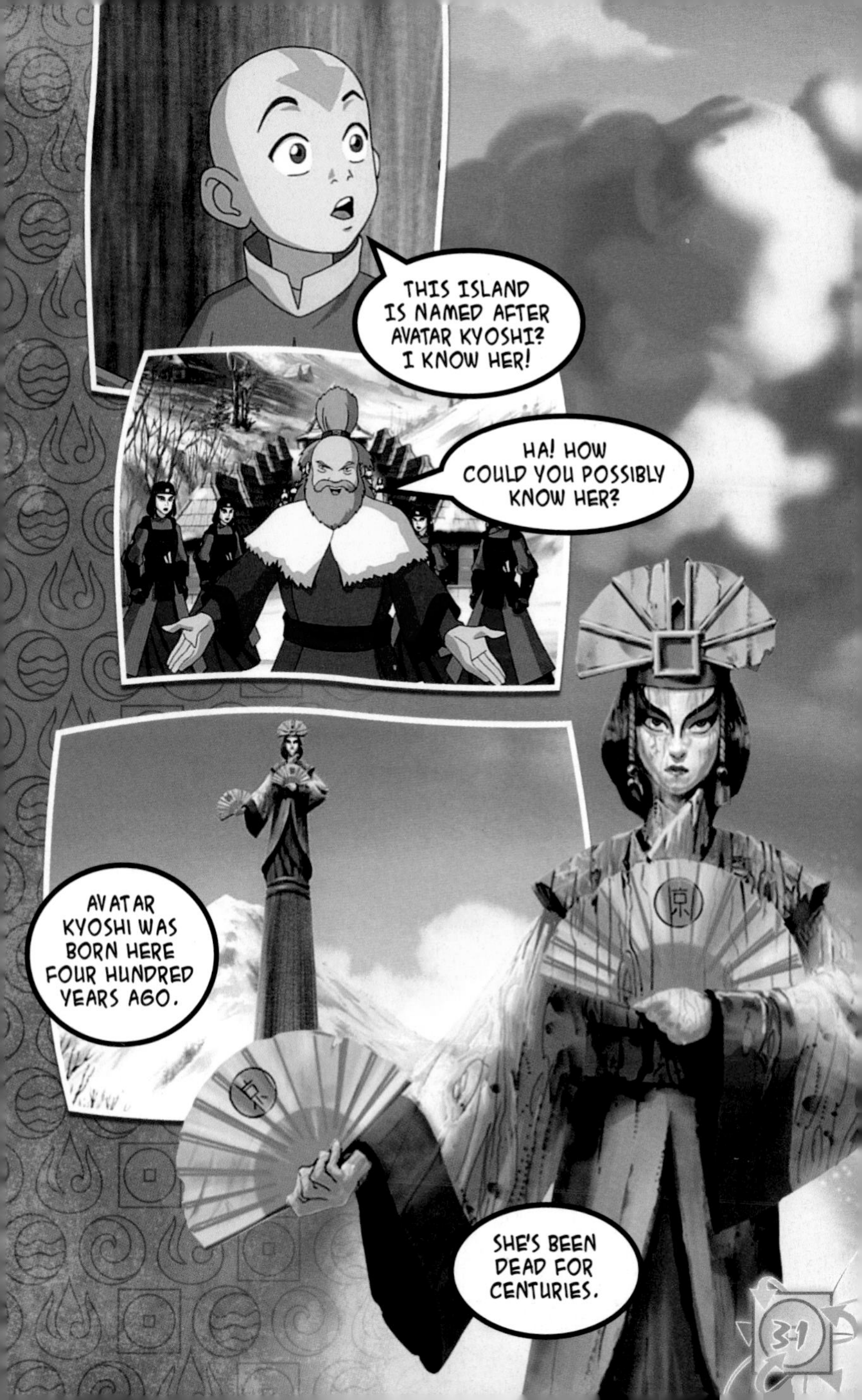
THIS ISLAND IS NAMED AFTER AVATAR KYOSHI? I KNOW HER!
HA! HOW COULD YOU POSSIBLY KNOW HER?
AVATAR KYOSHI WAS BORN HERE FOUR HUNDRED YEARS AGO.
SHE'S BEEN DEAD FOR CENTURIES.

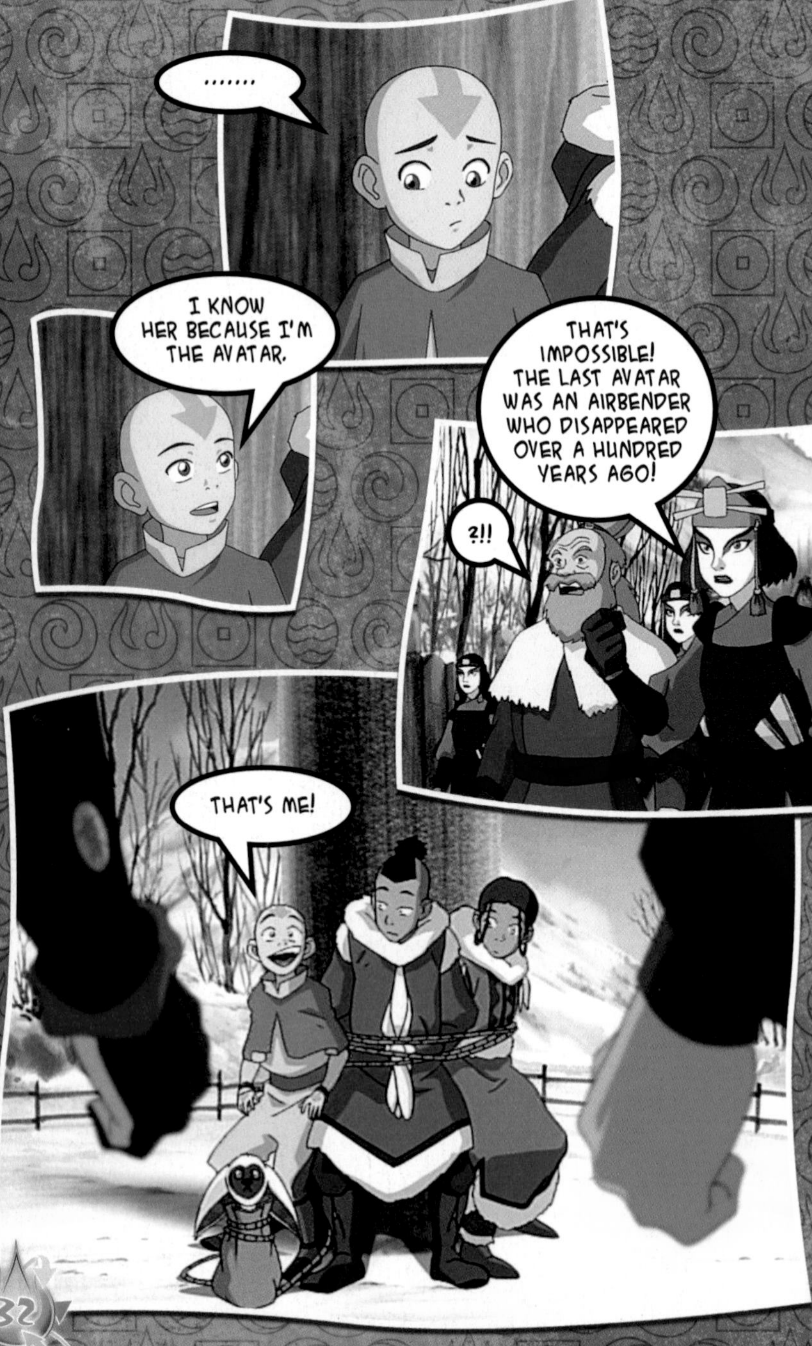
....
I KNOW HER BECAUSE I'M THE AVATAR.
THAT'S IMPOSSIBLE! THE LAST AVATAR WAS AN AIRBENDER WHO DISAPPEARED OVER A HUNDRED YEARS AGO!
?!!
THAT'S ME!

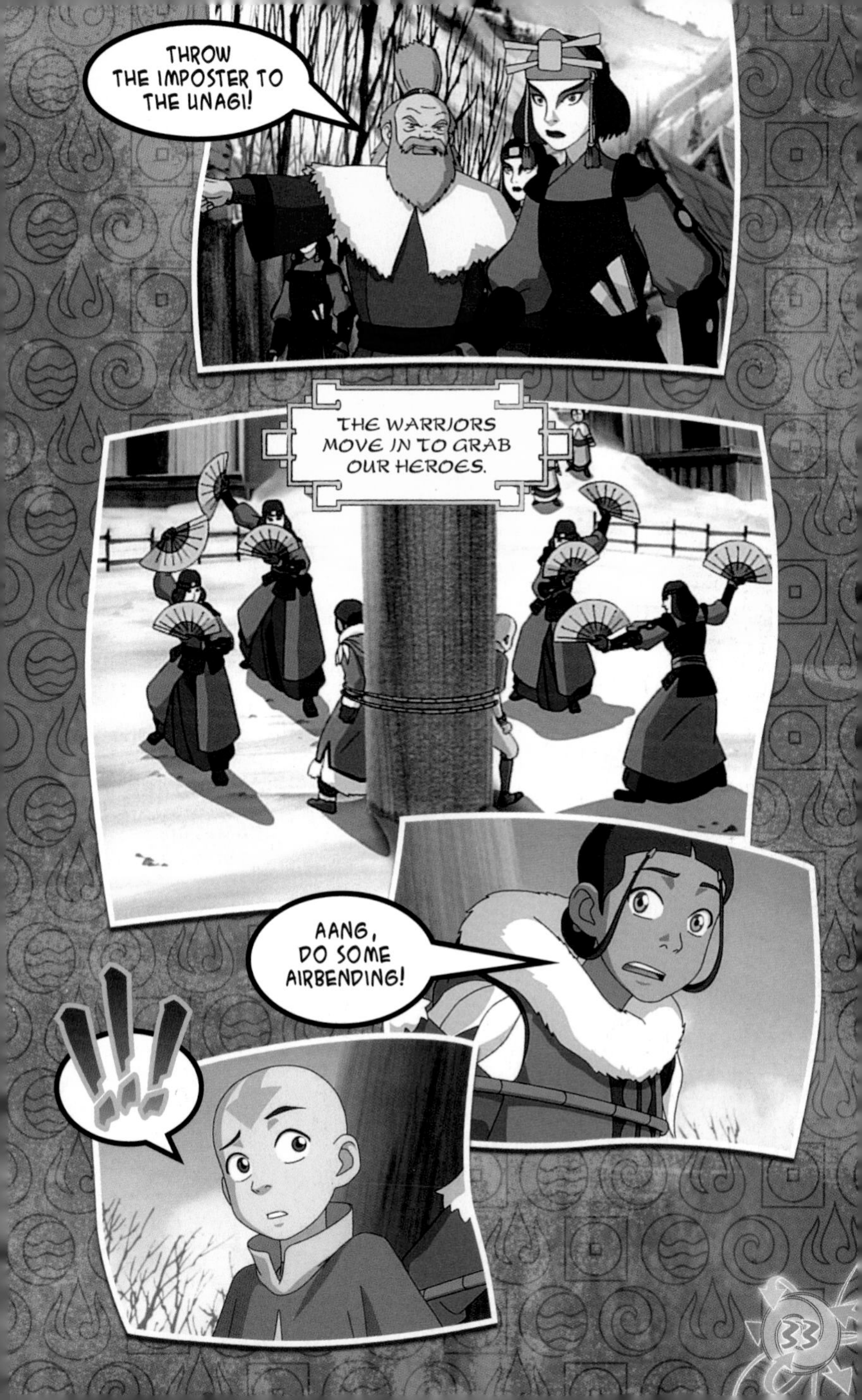
THROW THE IMPOSTER TO THE UNAGI!
THE WARRIORS MOVE IN TO GRAB OUR HEROES.
AANG, DO SOME AIRBENDING!
!!!
33

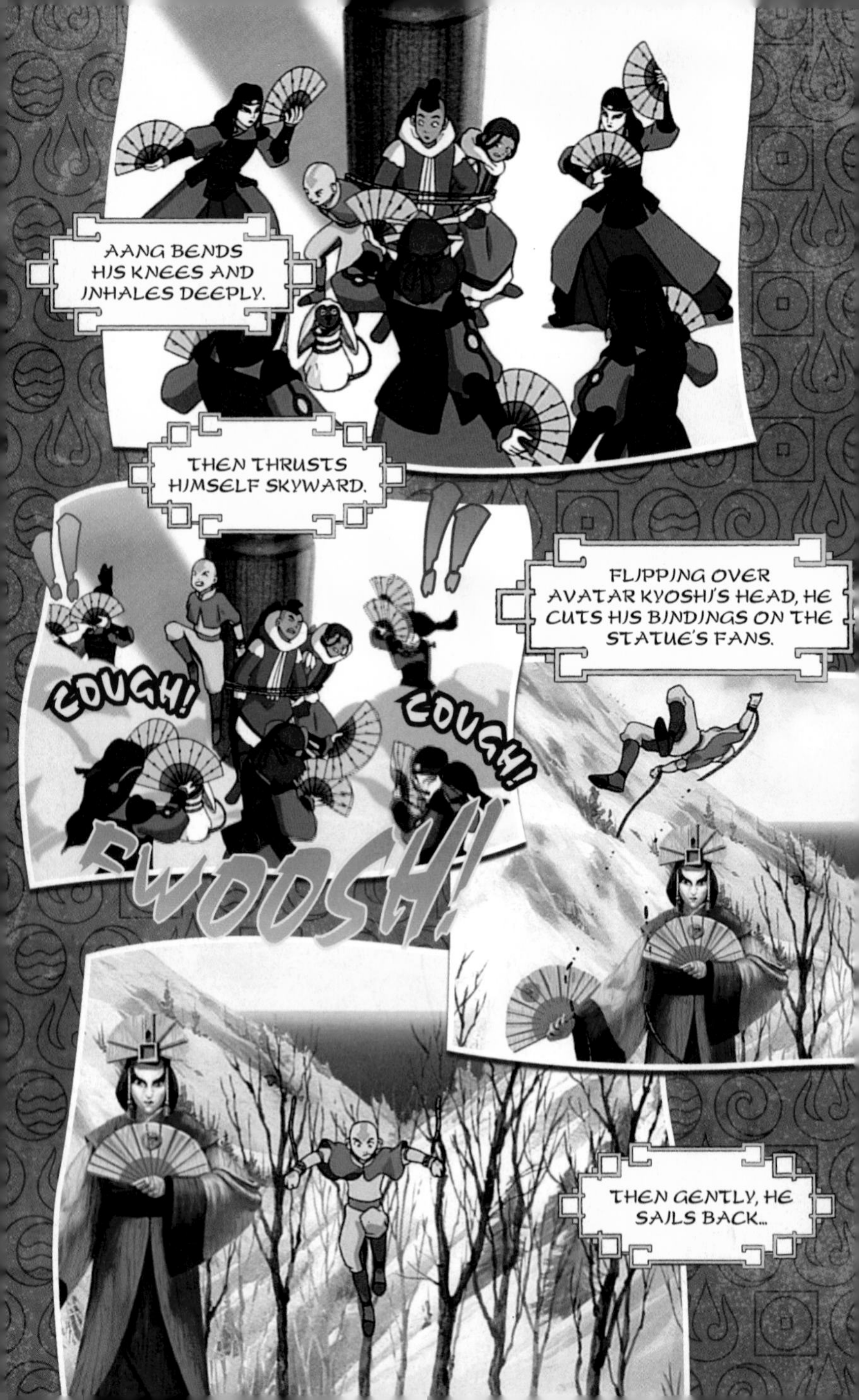
AANG BENDS HIS KNEES AND INHALES DEEPLY.
THEN THRUSTS HIMSELF SKYWARD.
!!
COUGH!
COUGH!
FWOOSH!
FLIPPING OVER AVATAR KYOSHI'S HEAD, HE CUTS HIS BINDINGS ON THE STATUE'S FANS.
THEN GENTLY, HE SAILS BACK...

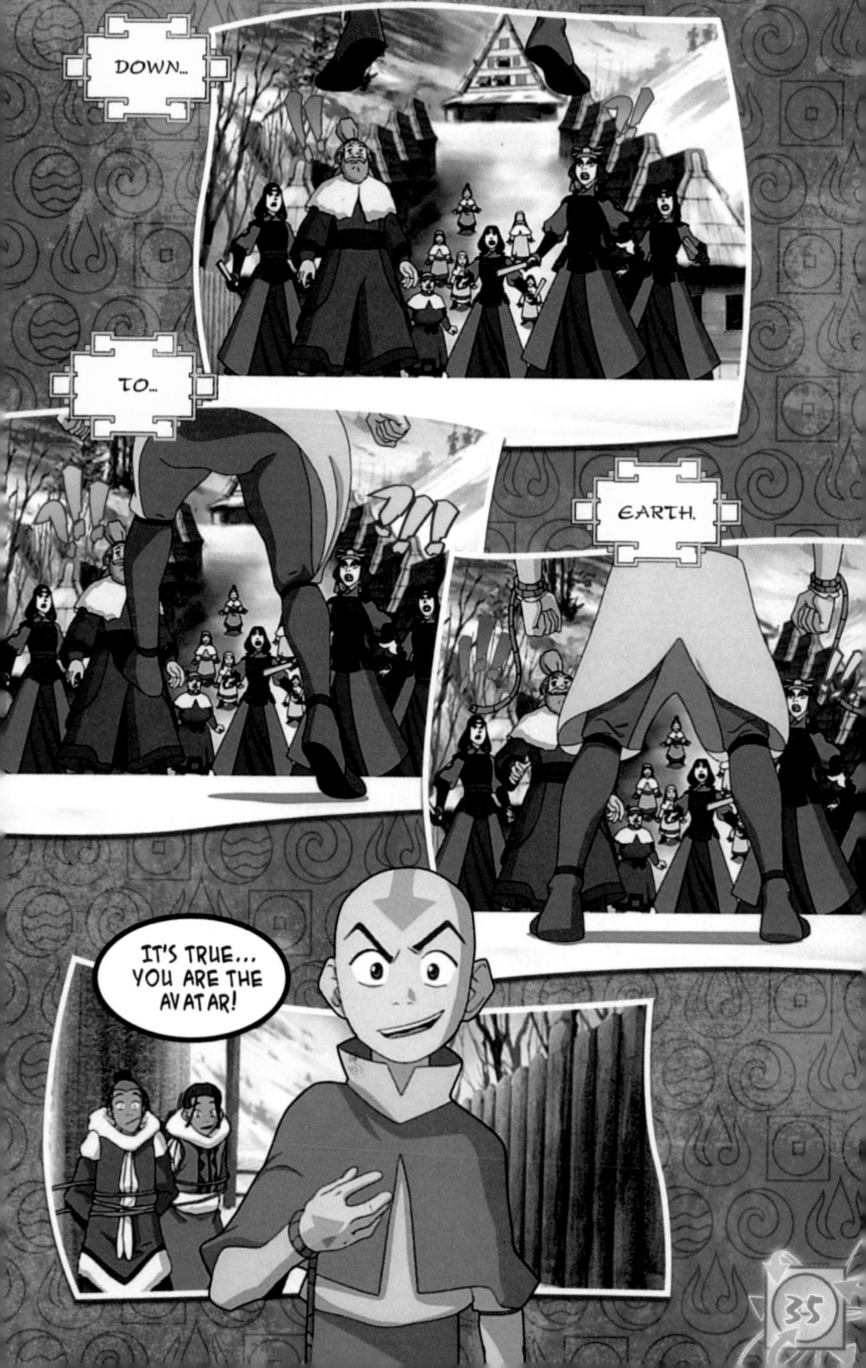
DOWN...
TO...
EARTH.
IT'S TRUE... YOU ARE THE AVATAR!

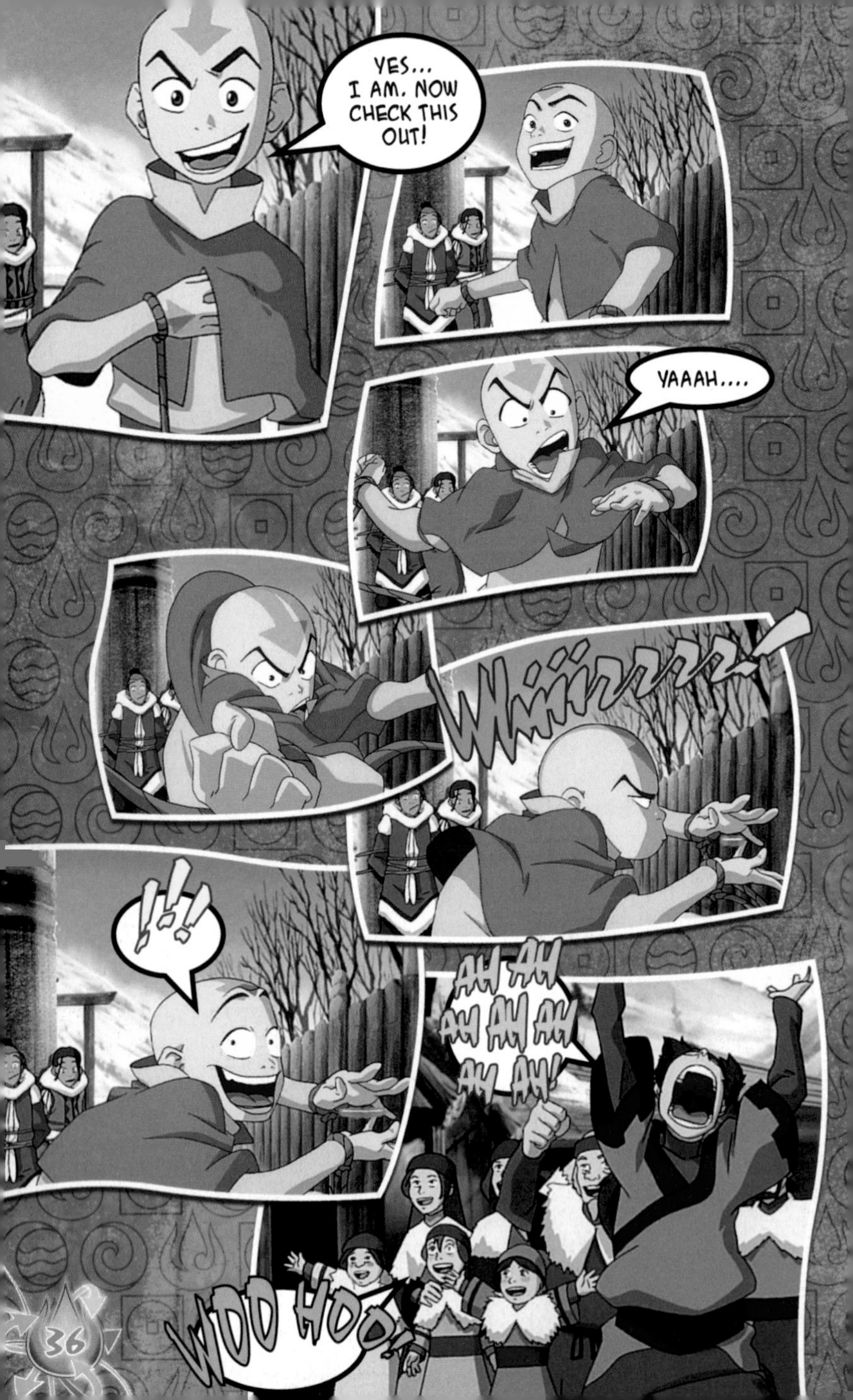
YES... I AM. NOW CHECK THIS OUT!
YAAAH....
WHIIIRRRR!
!!!
AH AH AH AH AH AH AH!
WOO HOO!

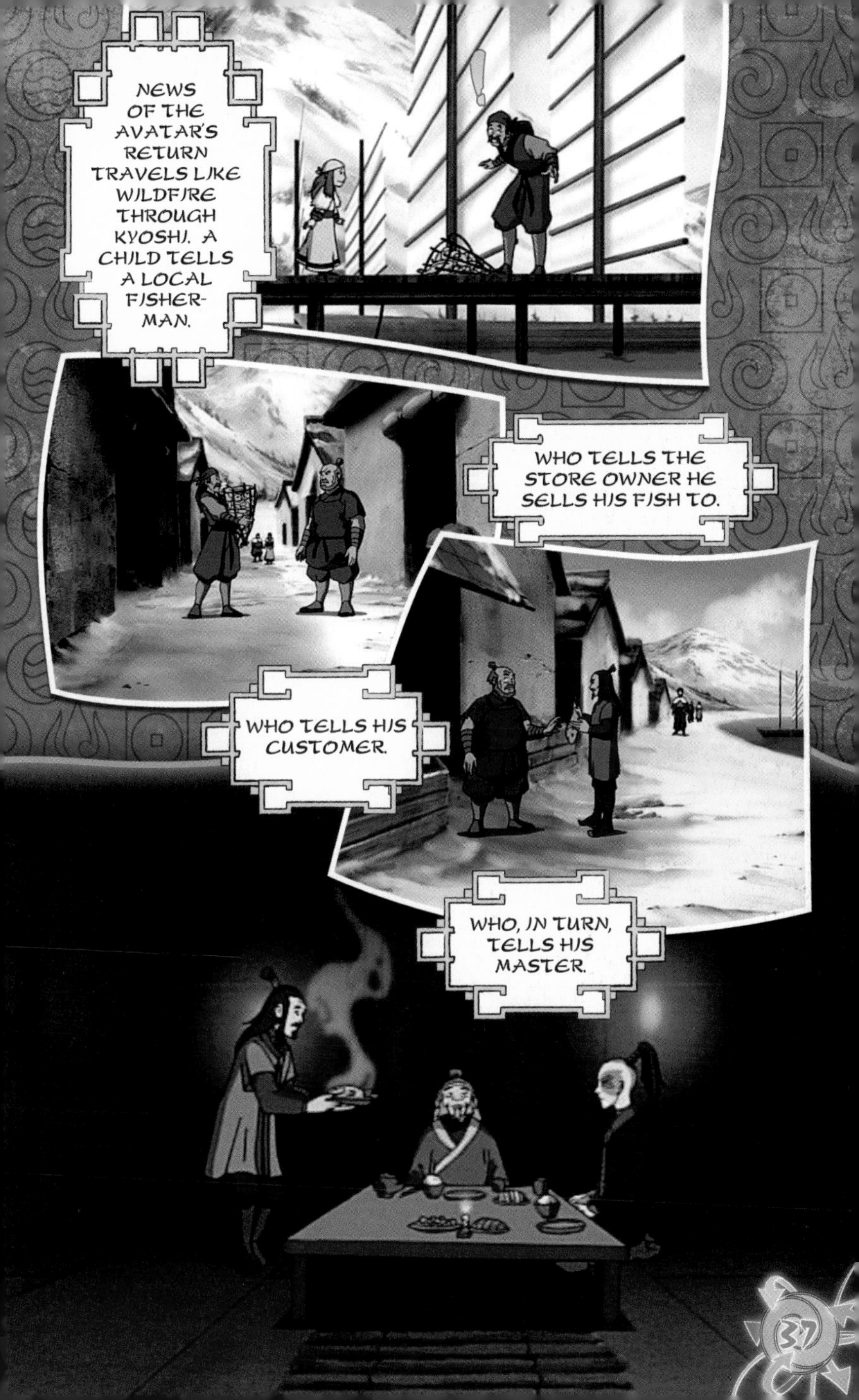
NEWS OF THE AVATAR'S RETURN TRAVELS LIKE WILDFIRE THROUGH KYOSHI. A CHILD TELLS A LOCAL FISHER-MAN.
WHO TELLS THE STORE OWNER HE SELLS HIS FISH TO.
WHO TELLS HIS CUSTOMER.
WHO, IN TURN, TELLS HIS MASTER.

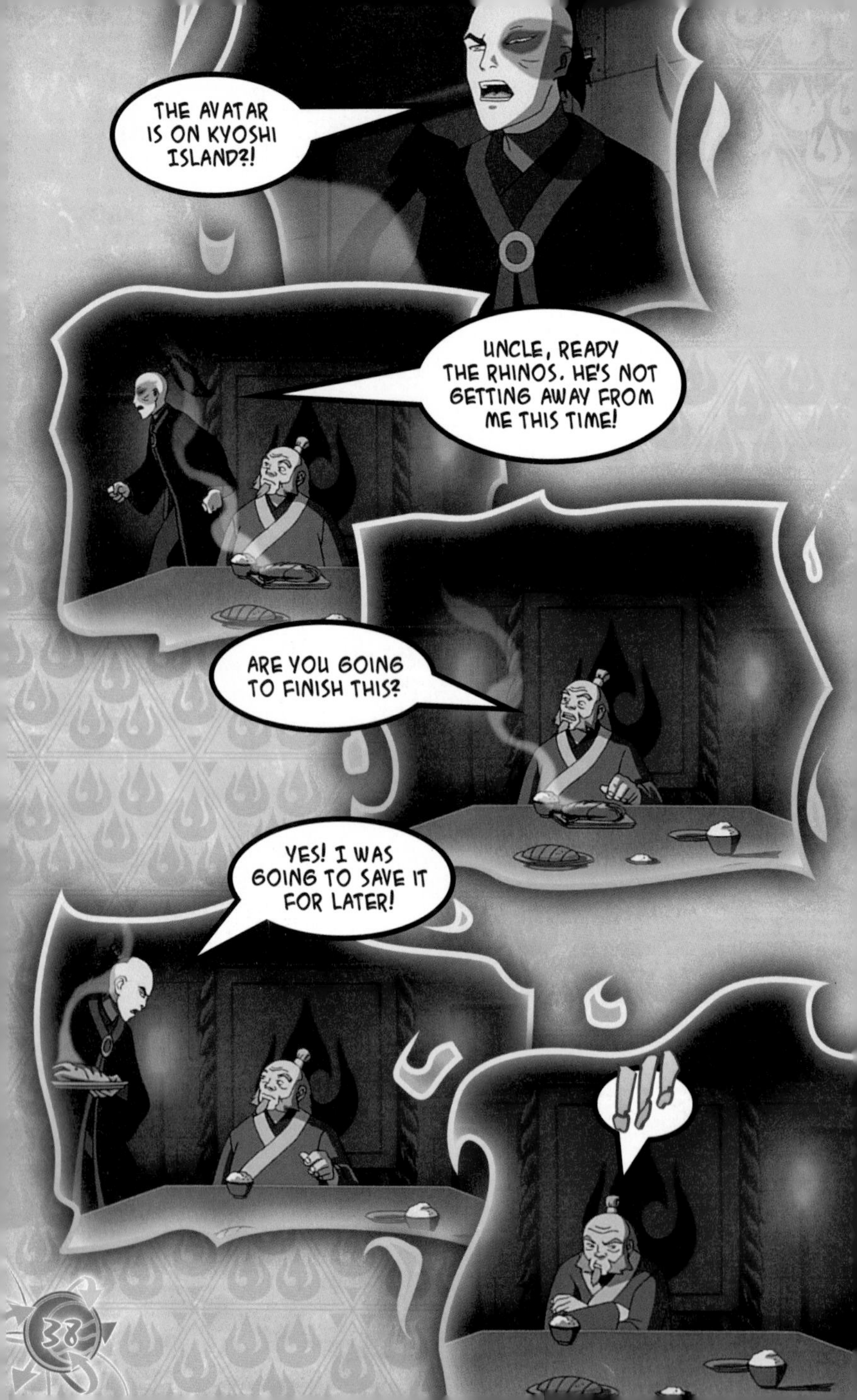

THE AVATAR IS ON KYOSHI ISLAND?!
UNCLE, READY THE RHINOS. HE'S NOT GETTING AWAY FROM ME THIS TIME!
ARE YOU GOING TO FINISH THIS?
YES! I WAS GOING TO SAVE IT FOR LATER!

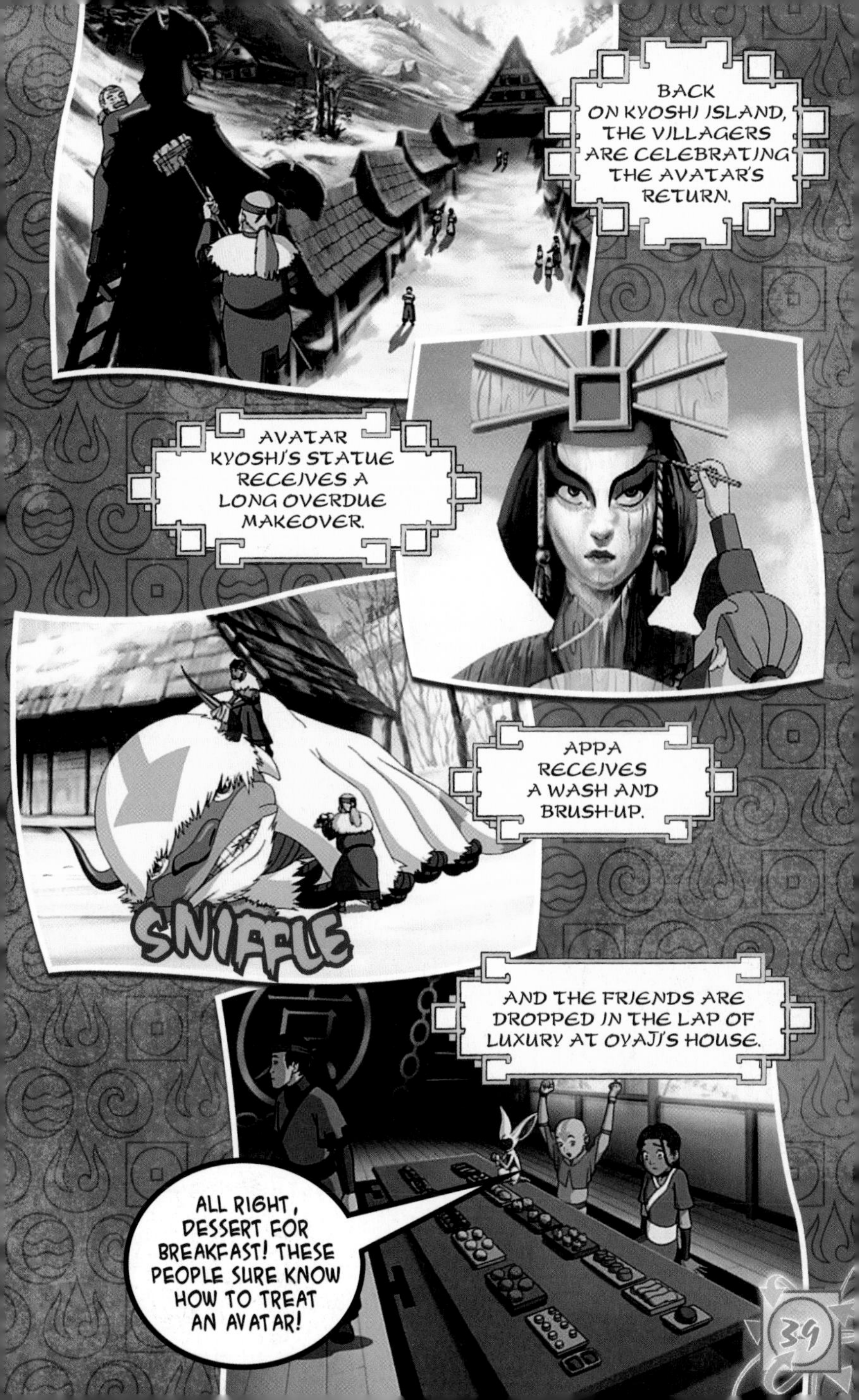
BACK ON KYOSHI ISLAND, THE VILLAGERS ARE CELEBRATING THE AVATAR'S RETURN.
AVATAR KYOSHI'S STATUE RECEIVES A LONG OVERDUE MAKEOVER.
APPA RECEIVES A WASH AND BRUSH-UP.
SNIFFLE
AND THE FRIENDS ARE DROPPED IN THE LAP OF LUXURY AT OYAJI'S HOUSE.
ALL RIGHT, DESSERT FOR BREAKFAST! THESE PEOPLE SURE KNOW HOW TO TREAT AN AVATAR!

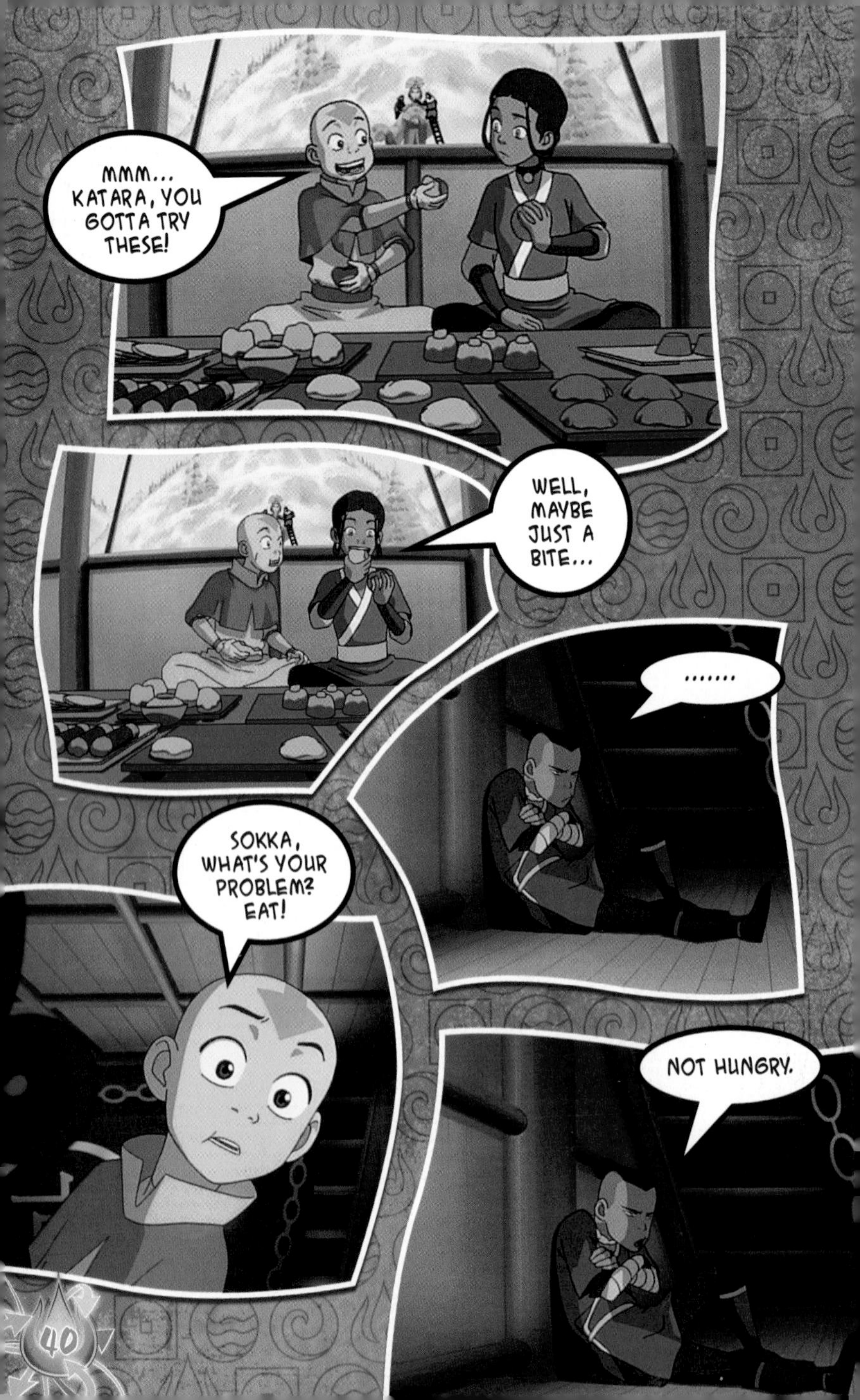
MMM... KATARA, YOU GOTTA TRY THESE!
WELL, MAYBE JUST A BITE...
....
SOKKA, WHAT'S YOUR PROBLEM? EAT!
NOT HUNGRY.

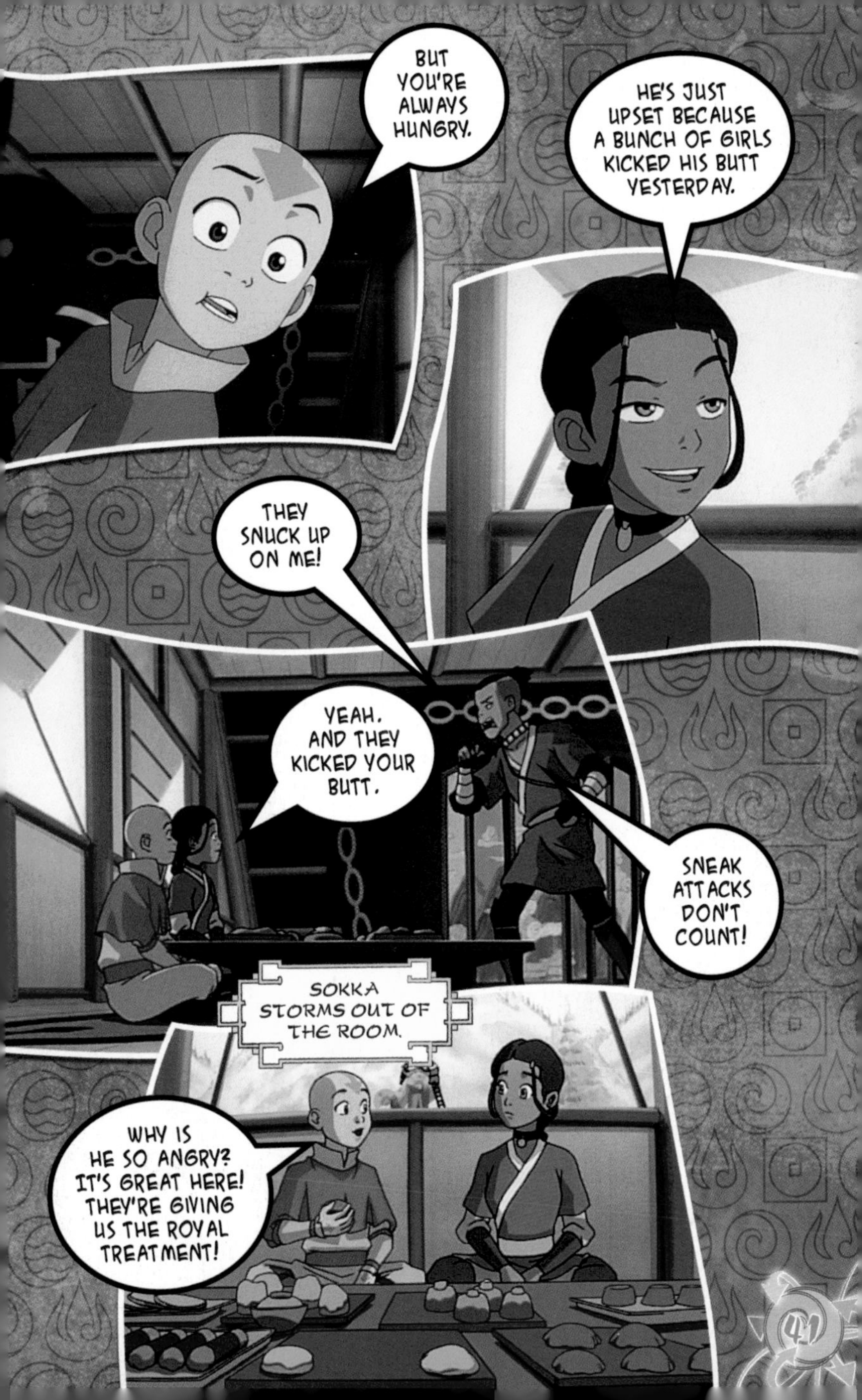
BUT YOU'RE ALWAYS HUNGRY.
HE'S JUST UPSET BECAUSE A BUNCH OF GIRLS KICKED HIS BUTT YESTERDAY.
THEY SNUCK UP ON ME!
YEAH. AND THEY KICKED YOUR BUTT.
SNEAK ATTACKS DON'T COUNT!
SOKKA STORMS OUT OF THE ROOM.
WHY IS HE SO ANGRY? IT'S GREAT HERE! THEY'RE GIVING US THE ROYAL TREATMENT!

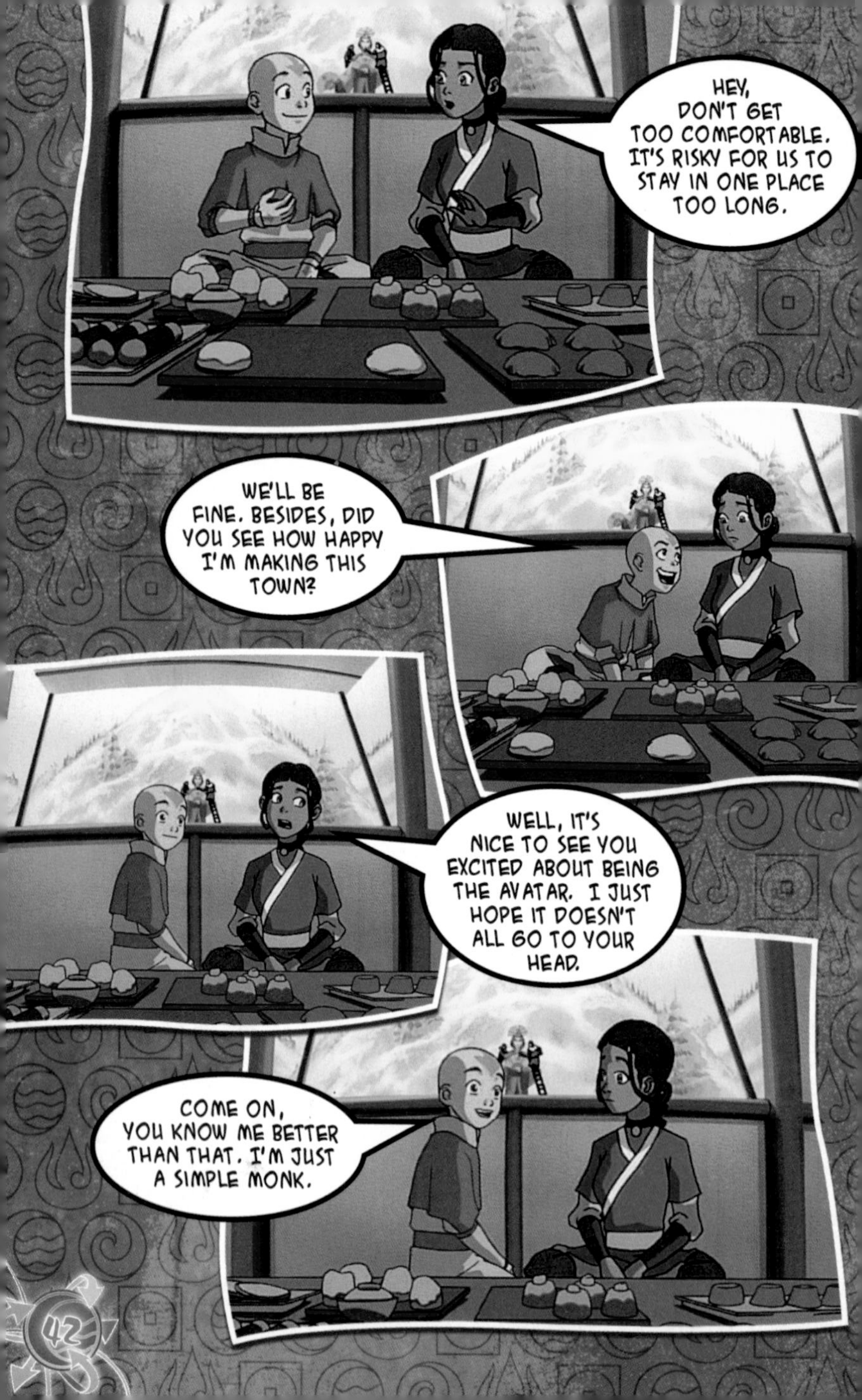
HEY, DON'T GET TOO COMFORTABLE. IT'S RISKY FOR US TO STAY IN ONE PLACE TOO LONG.
WE'LL BE FINE. BESIDES, DID YOU SEE HOW HAPPY I'M MAKING THIS TOWN?
WELL, IT'S NICE TO SEE YOU EXCITED ABOUT BEING THE AVATAR. I JUST HOPE IT DOESN'T ALL GO TO YOUR HEAD.
COME ON, YOU KNOW ME BETTER THAN THAT. I'M JUST A SIMPLE MONK.

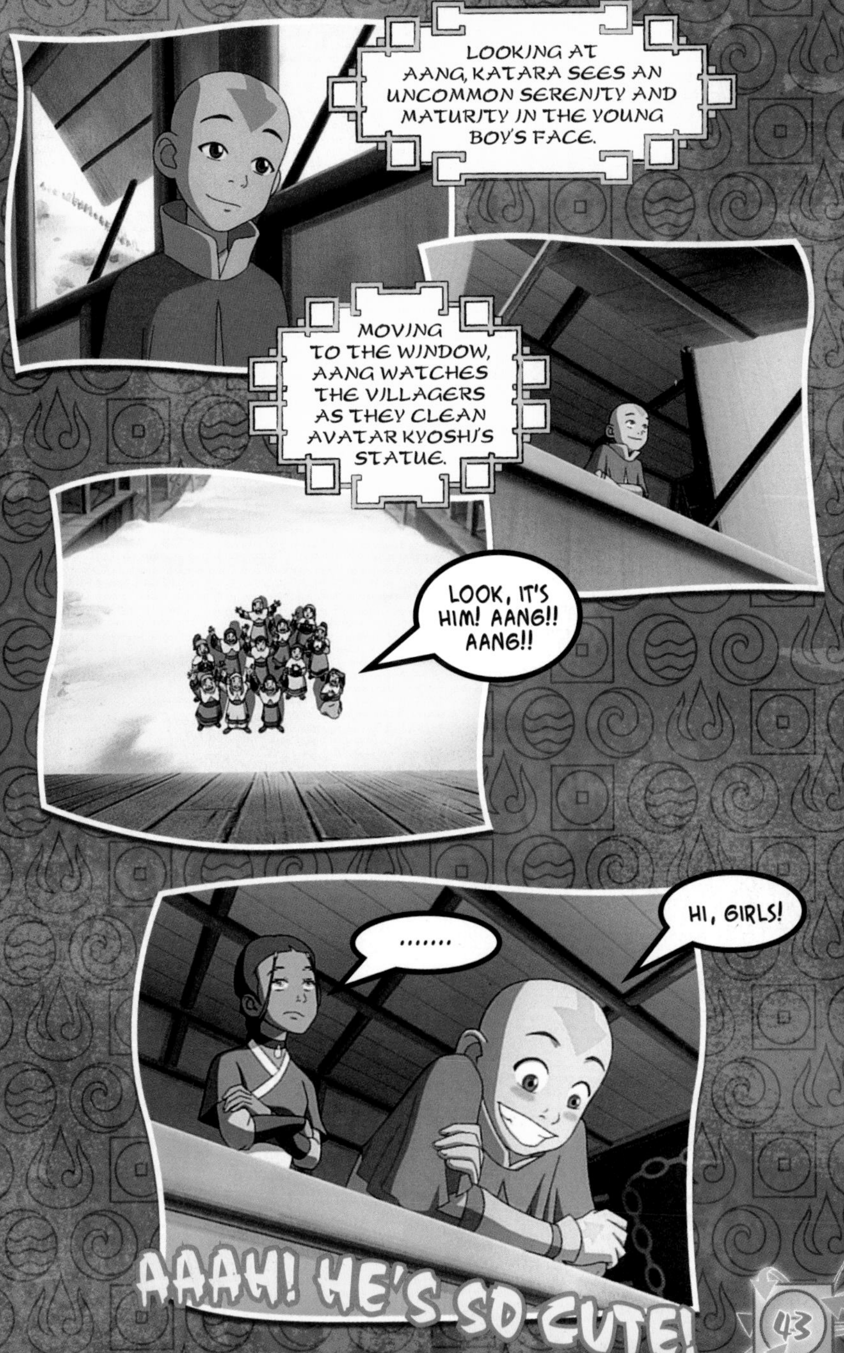
LOOKING AT AANG, KATARA SEES AN UNCOMMON SERENITY AND MATURITY IN THE YOUNG BOY'S FACE.
MOVING TO THE WINDOW, AANG WATCHES THE VILLAGERS AS THEY CLEAN AVATAR KYOSHI'S STATUE.
LOOK, IT'S HIM! AANG!! AANG!!
....
HI, GIRLS!
AAAH! HE'S SO CUTE!

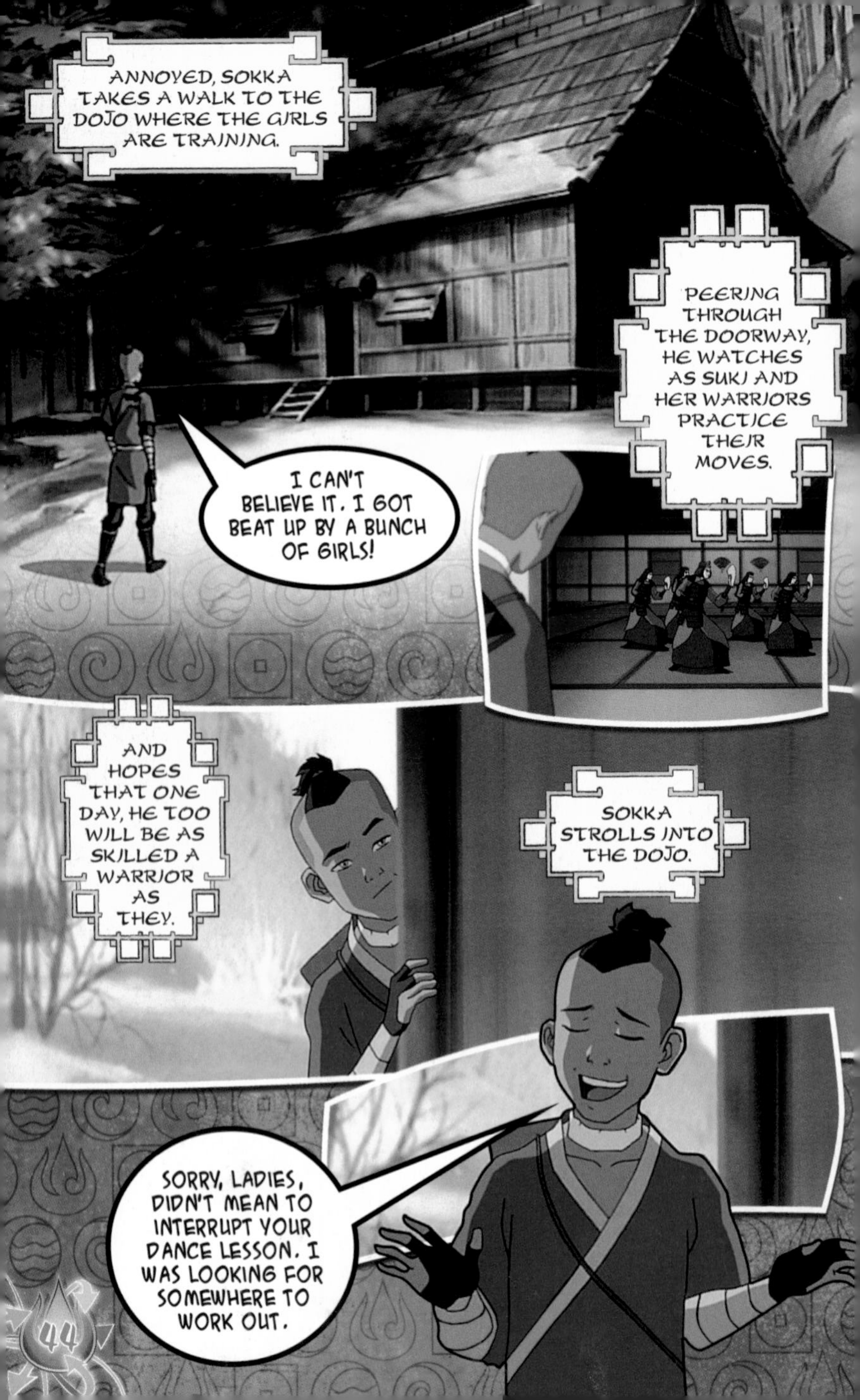
ANNOYED, SOKKA TAKES A WALK TO THE DOJO WHERE THE GIRLS ARE TRAINING.
I CAN'T BELIEVE IT. I GOT BEAT UP BY A BUNCH OF GIRLS!
PEERING THROUGH THE DOORWAY, HE WATCHES AS SUKI AND HER WARRIORS PRACTICE THEIR MOVES.
AND HOPES THAT ONE DAY, HE TOO WILL BE AS SKILLED A WARRIOR AS THEY.
SOKKA STROLLS INTO THE DOJO.
SORRY, LADIES, DIDN'T MEAN TO INTERRUPT YOUR DANCE LESSON. I WAS LOOKING FOR SOMEWHERE TO WORK OUT.

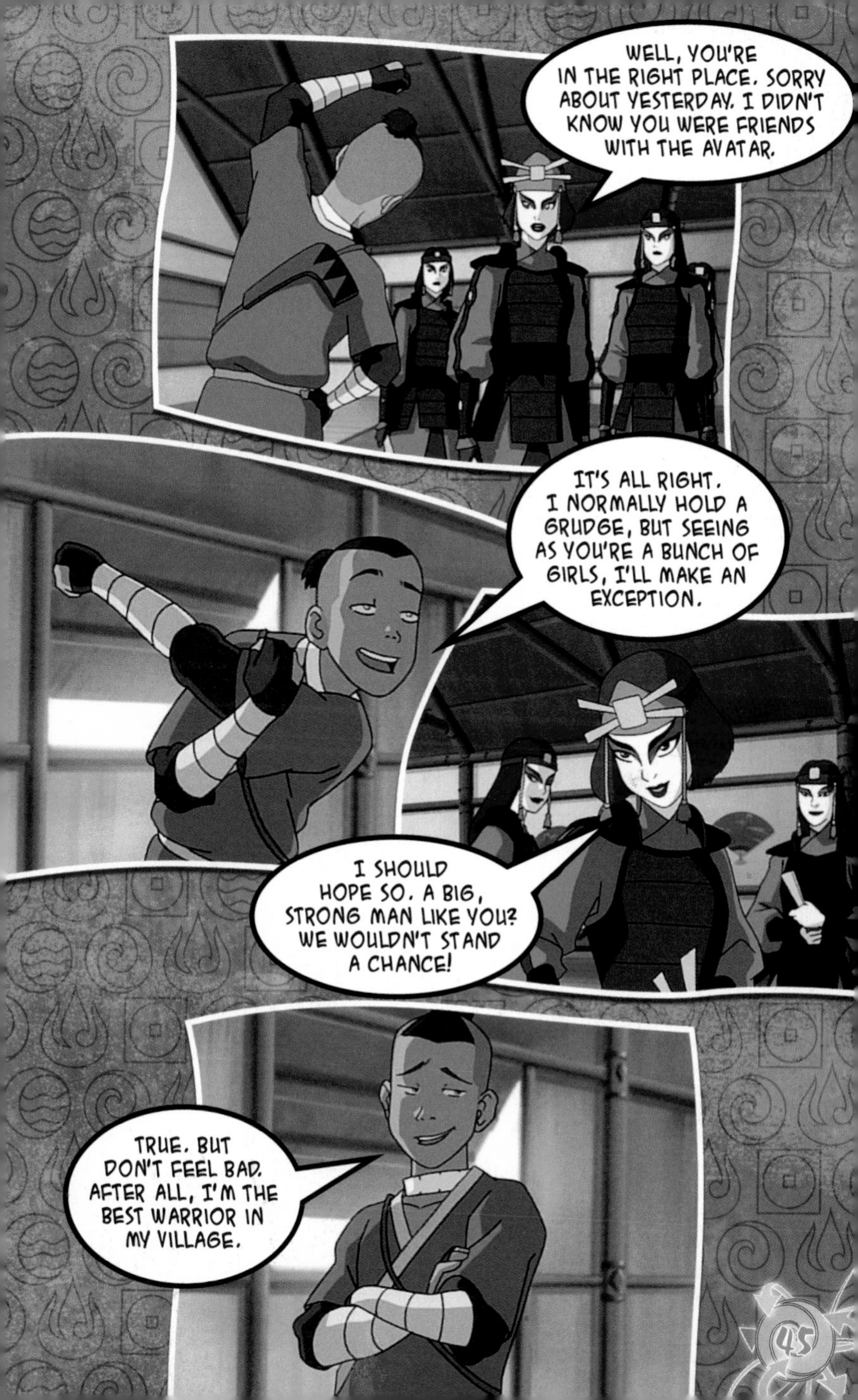
WELL, YOU'RE IN THE RIGHT PLACE. SORRY ABOUT YESTERDAY. I DIDN'T KNOW YOU WERE FRIENDS WITH THE AVATAR.
IT'S ALL RIGHT. I NORMALLY HOLD A GRUDGE, BUT SEEING AS YOU'RE A BUNCH OF GIRLS, I'LL MAKE AN EXCEPTION.
I SHOULD HOPE SO. A BIG, STRONG MAN LIKE YOU? WE WOULDN'T STAND A CHANCE!
TRUE. BUT DON'T FEEL BAD. AFTER ALL, I'M THE BEST WARRIOR IN MY VILLAGE.

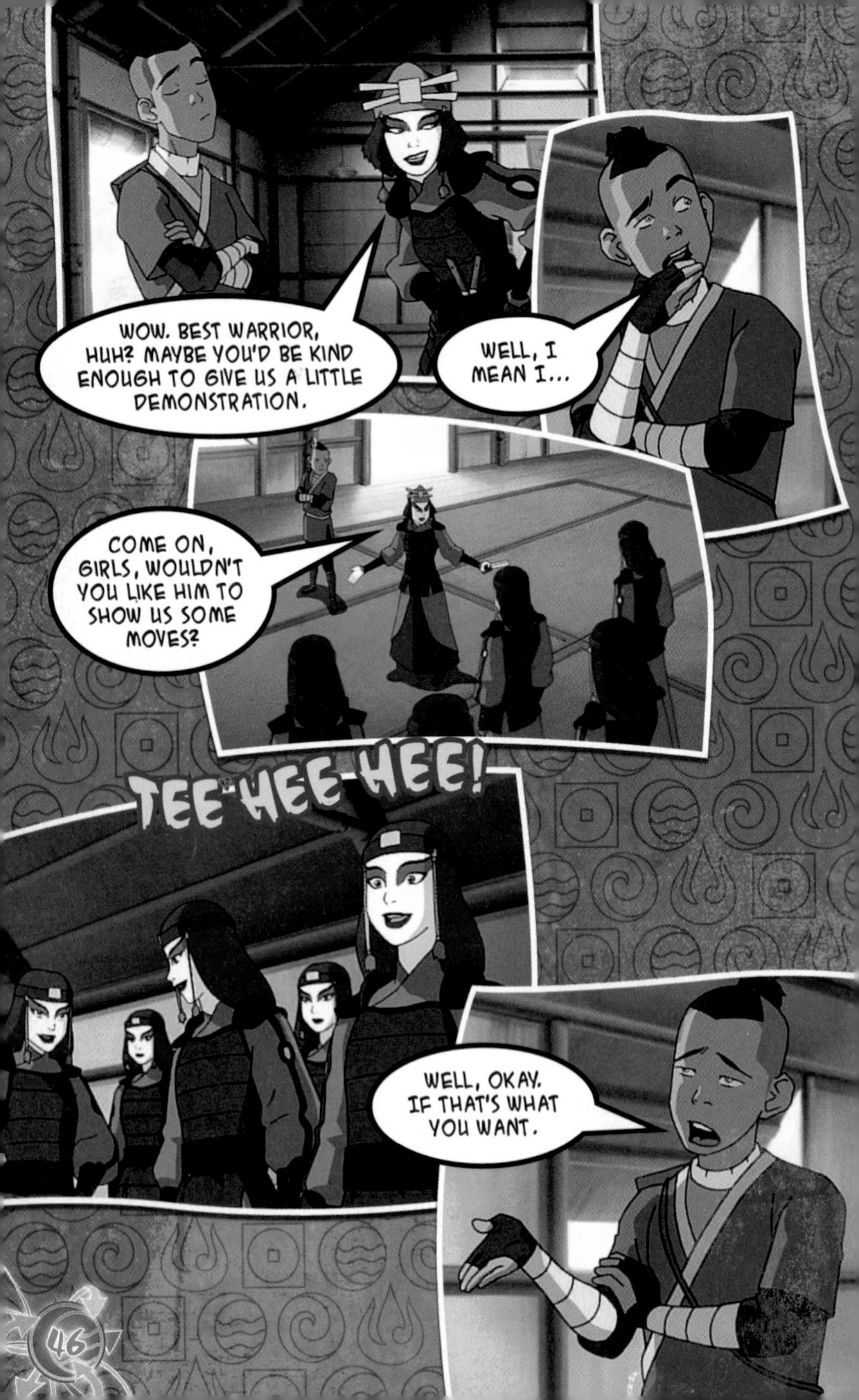
WOW. BEST WARRIOR, HUH? MAYBE YOU'D BE KIND ENOUGH TO GIVE US A LITTLE DEMONSTRATION.
WELL, I MEAN I...
COME ON, GIRLS, WOULDN'T YOU LIKE HIM TO SHOW US SOME MOVES?
TEE HEE HEE!
WELL, OKAY. IF THAT'S WHAT YOU WANT.

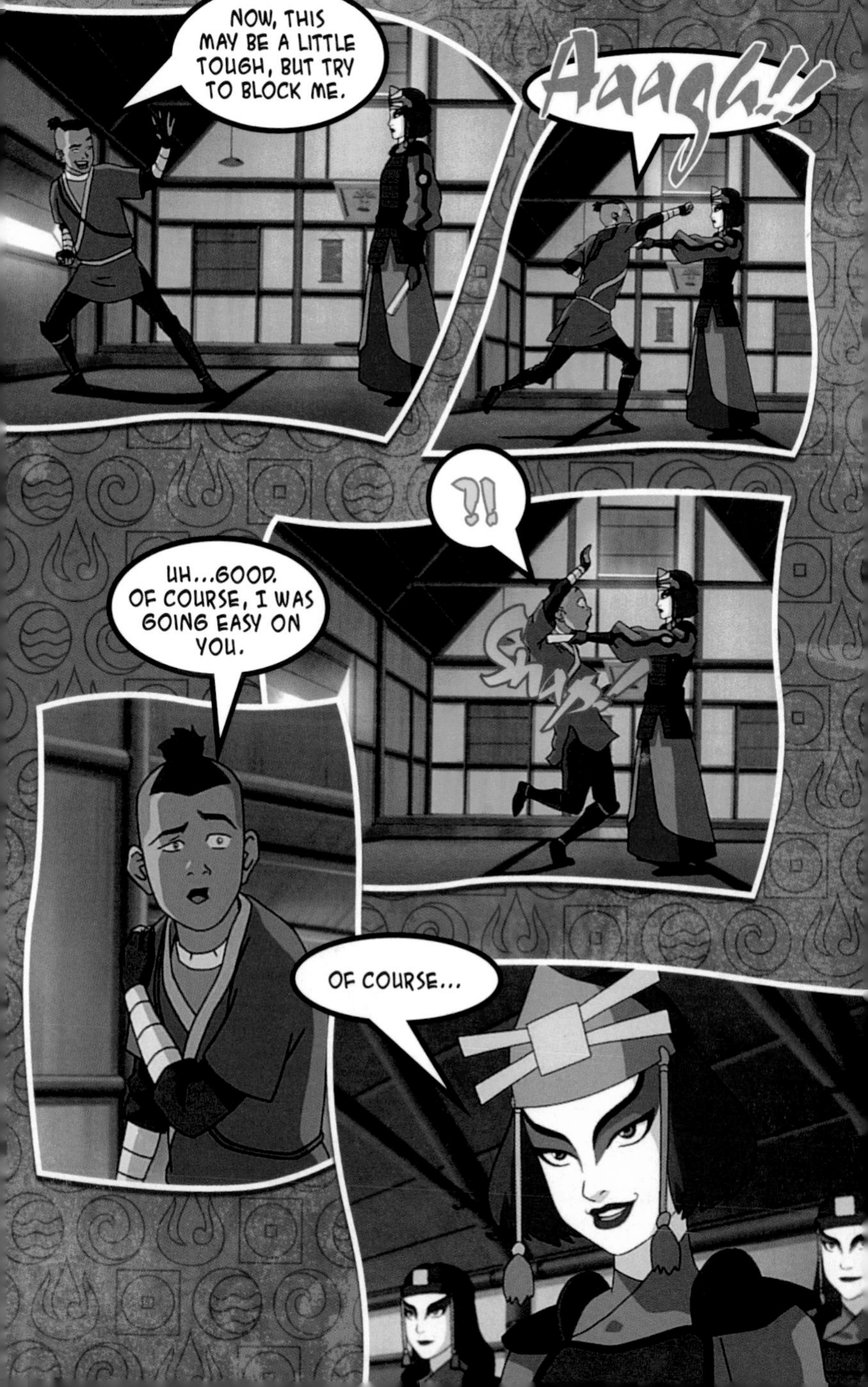

NOW, THIS MAY BE A LITTLE TOUGH, BUT TRY TO BLOCK ME.
Aaagh!!
?!
Snap!
UH...GOOD. OF COURSE, I WAS GOING EASY ON YOU.
OF COURSE...

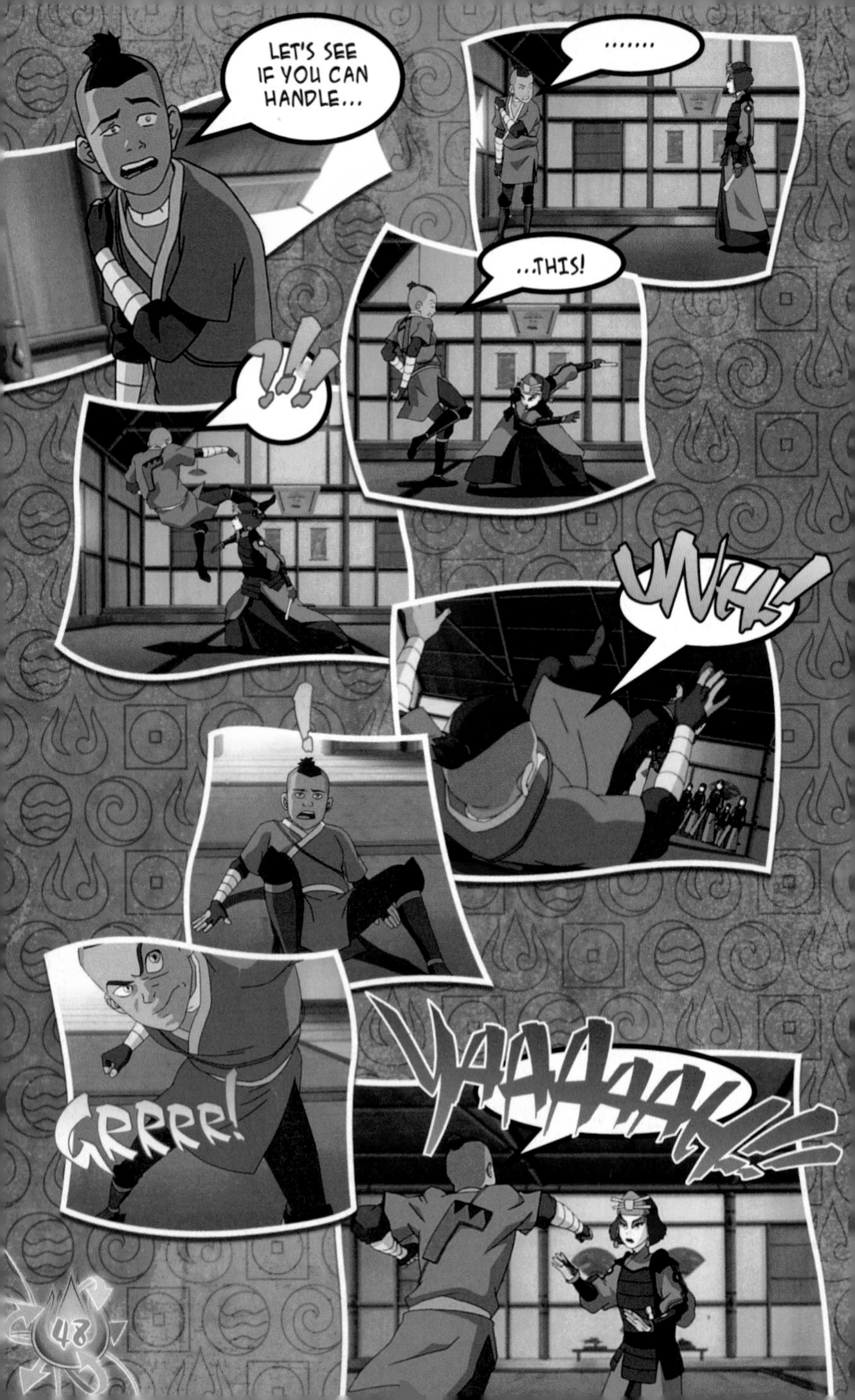
LET'S SEE IF YOU CAN HANDLE...
....
...THIS!
!!
UNH!
!
GRRRR!
YAAAAAH!!!

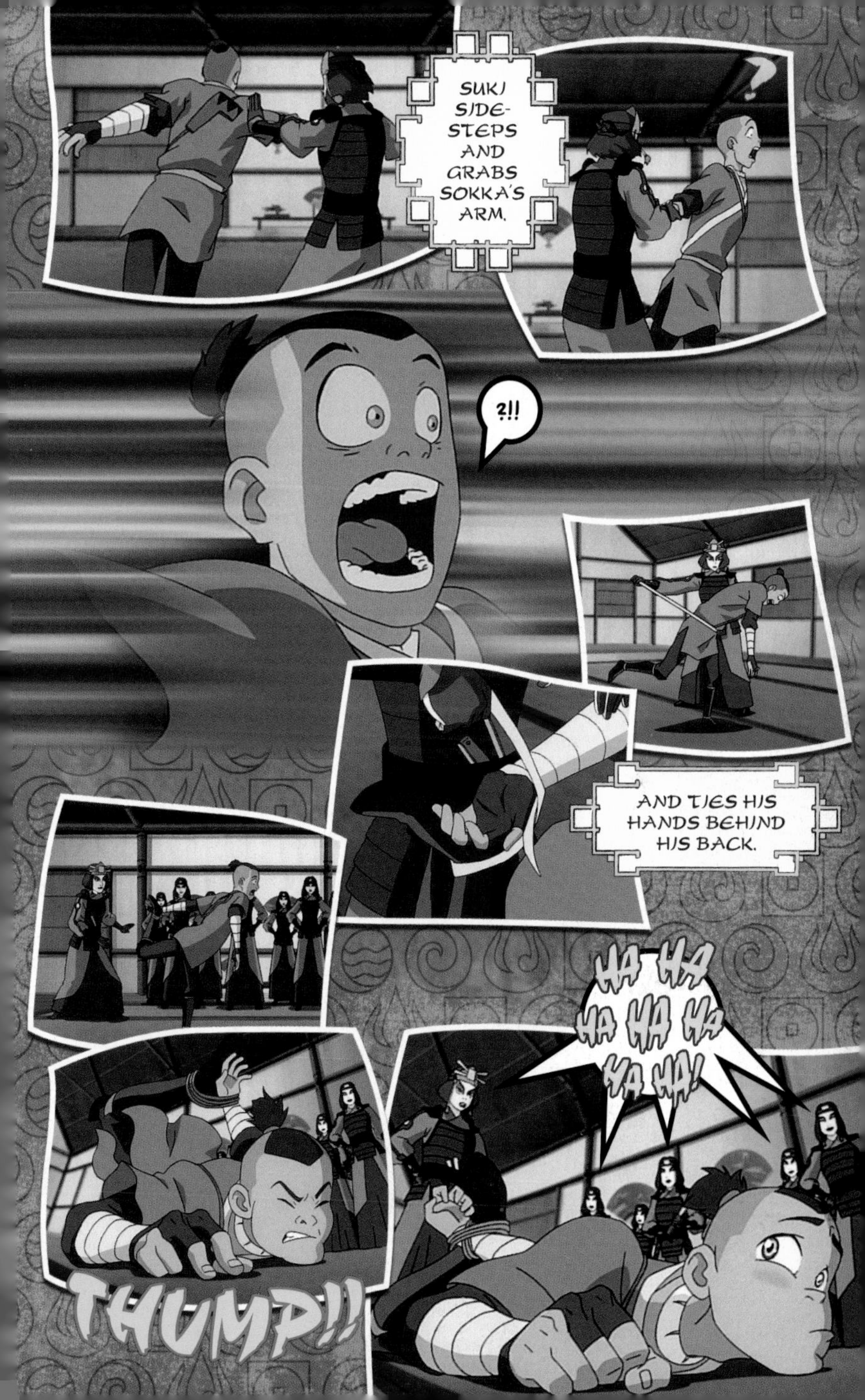
SUKI SIDE-STEPS AND GRABS SOKKA'S ARM.
?!!
AND TIES HIS HANDS BEHIND HIS BACK.
HA HA HA HA HA HA HA!
THUMP!!

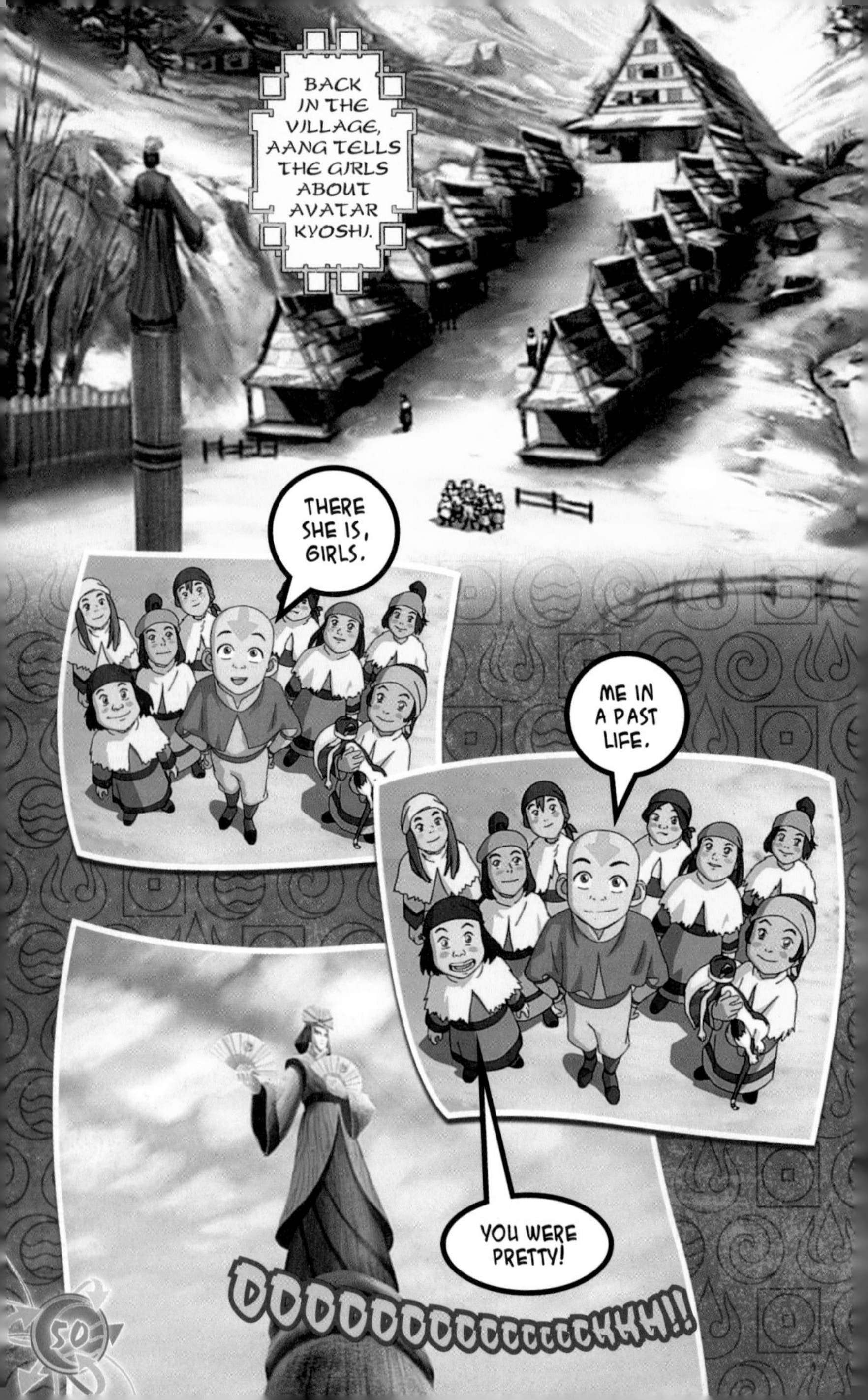
BACK IN THE VILLAGE, AANG TELLS THE GIRLS ABOUT AVATAR KYOSHI.
THERE SHE IS, GIRLS.
ME IN A PAST LIFE.
YOU WERE PRETTY!
DDDDDDDDDDDEEEEEEEEECHHH!!

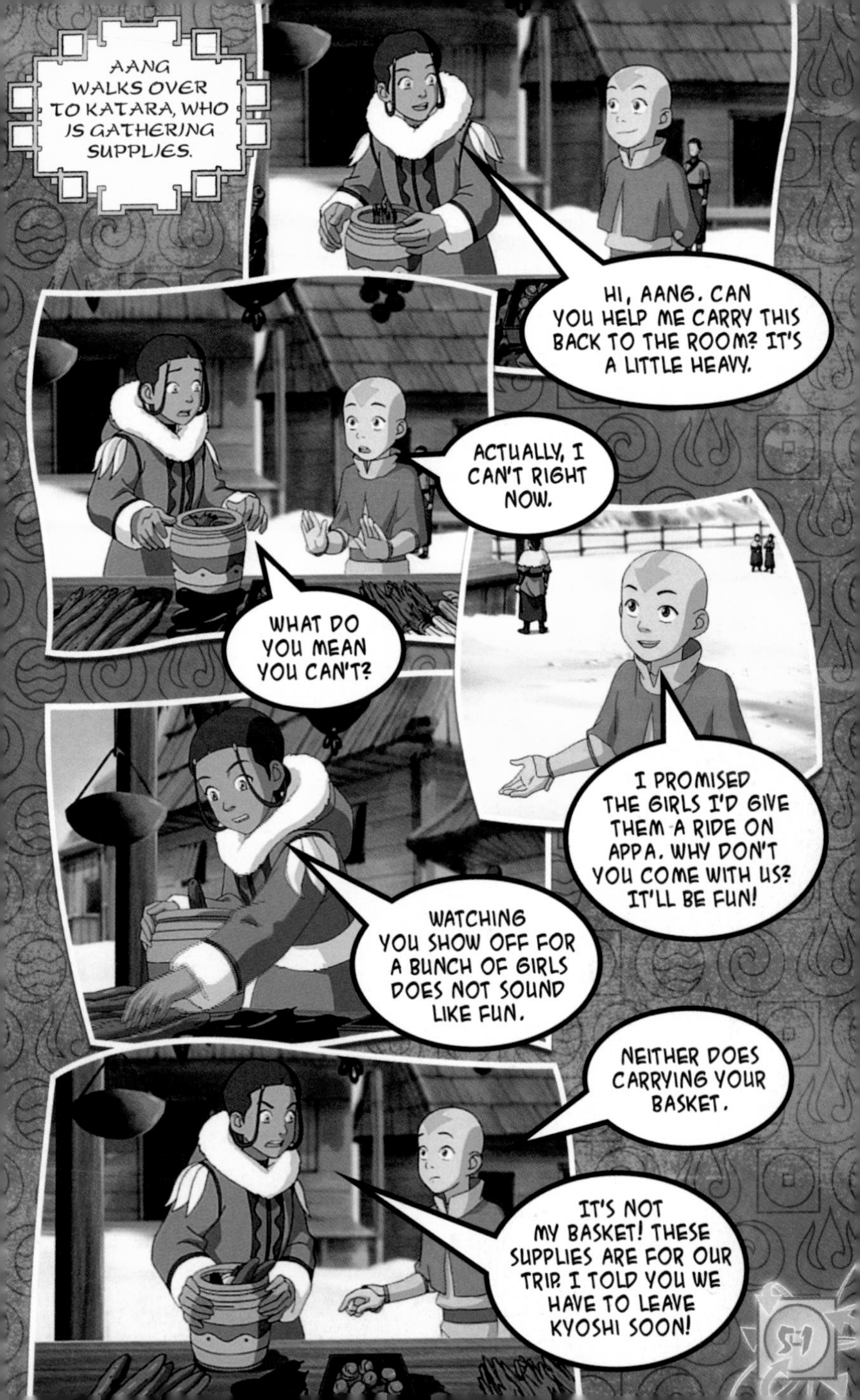
AANG WALKS OVER TO KATARA, WHO IS GATHERING SUPPLIES.
HI, AANG. CAN YOU HELP ME CARRY THIS BACK TO THE ROOM? IT'S A LITTLE HEAVY.
ACTUALLY, I CAN'T RIGHT NOW.
WHAT DO YOU MEAN YOU CAN'T?
I PROMISED THE GIRLS I'D GIVE THEM A RIDE ON APPA. WHY DON'T YOU COME WITH US? IT'LL BE FUN!
WATCHING YOU SHOW OFF FOR A BUNCH OF GIRLS DOES NOT SOUND LIKE FUN.
NEITHER DOES CARRYING YOUR BASKET.
IT'S NOT MY BASKET! THESE SUPPLIES ARE FOR OUR TRIP. I TOLD YOU WE HAVE TO LEAVE KYOSHI SOON!

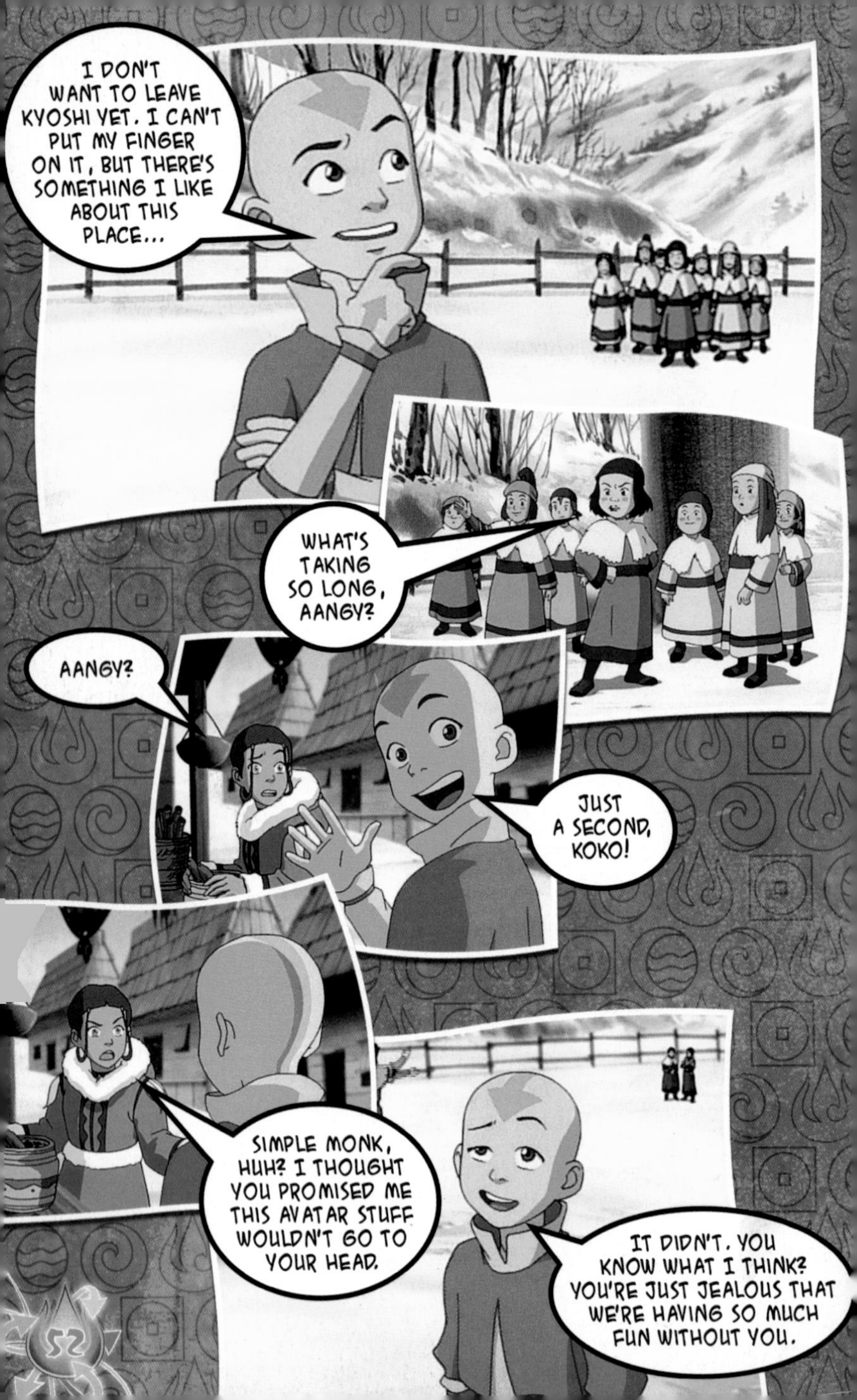
I DON'T WANT TO LEAVE KYOSHI YET. I CAN'T PUT MY FINGER ON IT, BUT THERE'S SOMETHING I LIKE ABOUT THIS PLACE...
WHAT'S TAKING SO LONG, AANGY?
AANGY?
JUST A SECOND, KOKO!
SIMPLE MONK, HUH? I THOUGHT YOU PROMISED ME THIS AVATAR STUFF WOULDN'T GO TO YOUR HEAD.
IT DIDN'T. YOU KNOW WHAT I THINK? YOU'RE JUST JEALOUS THAT WE'RE HAVING SO MUCH FUN WITHOUT YOU.
52

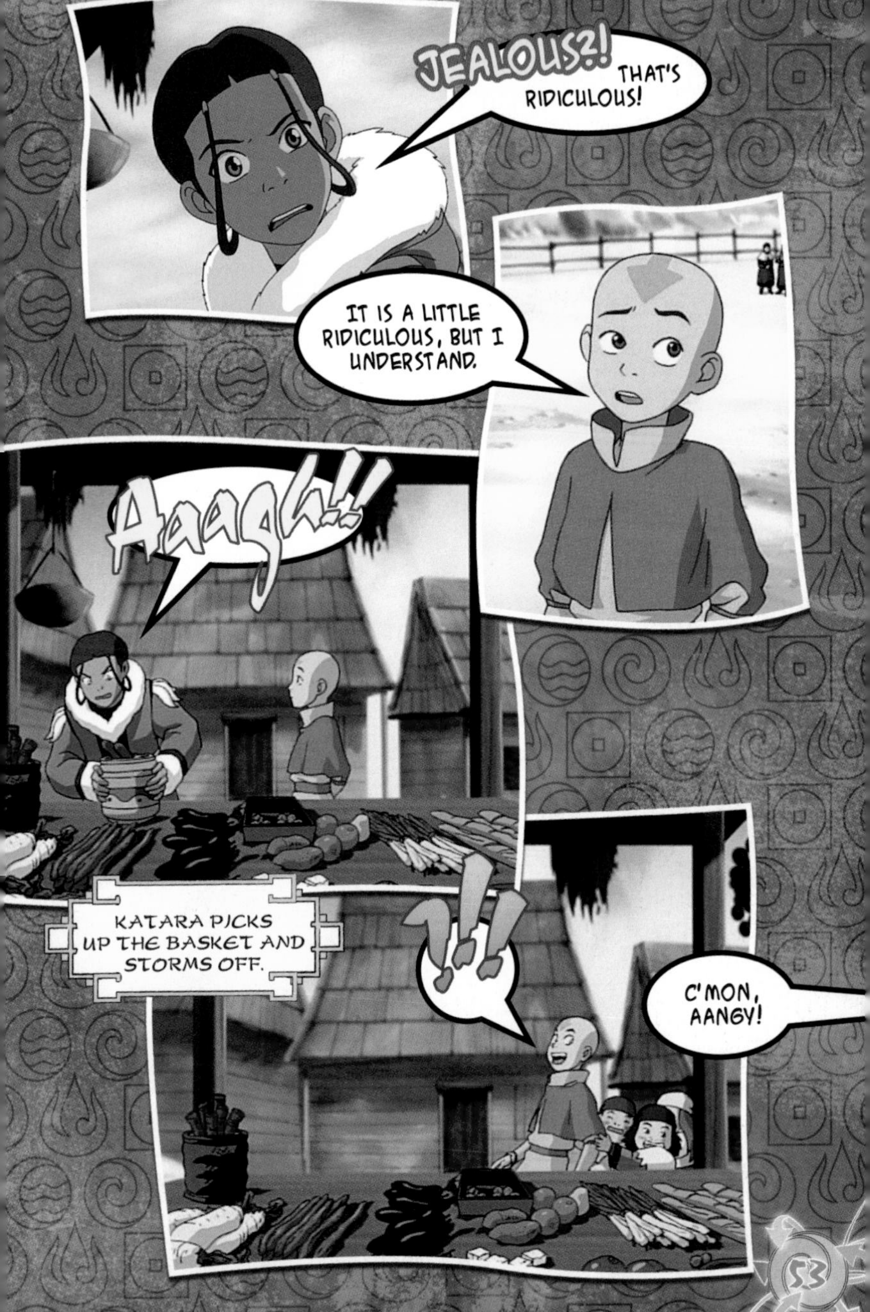
JEALOUS?! THAT'S RIDICULOUS!
IT IS A LITTLE RIDICULOUS, BUT I UNDERSTAND.
Aaagh!!
KATARA PICKS UP THE BASKET AND STORMS OFF.
!!
C'MON, AANGY!

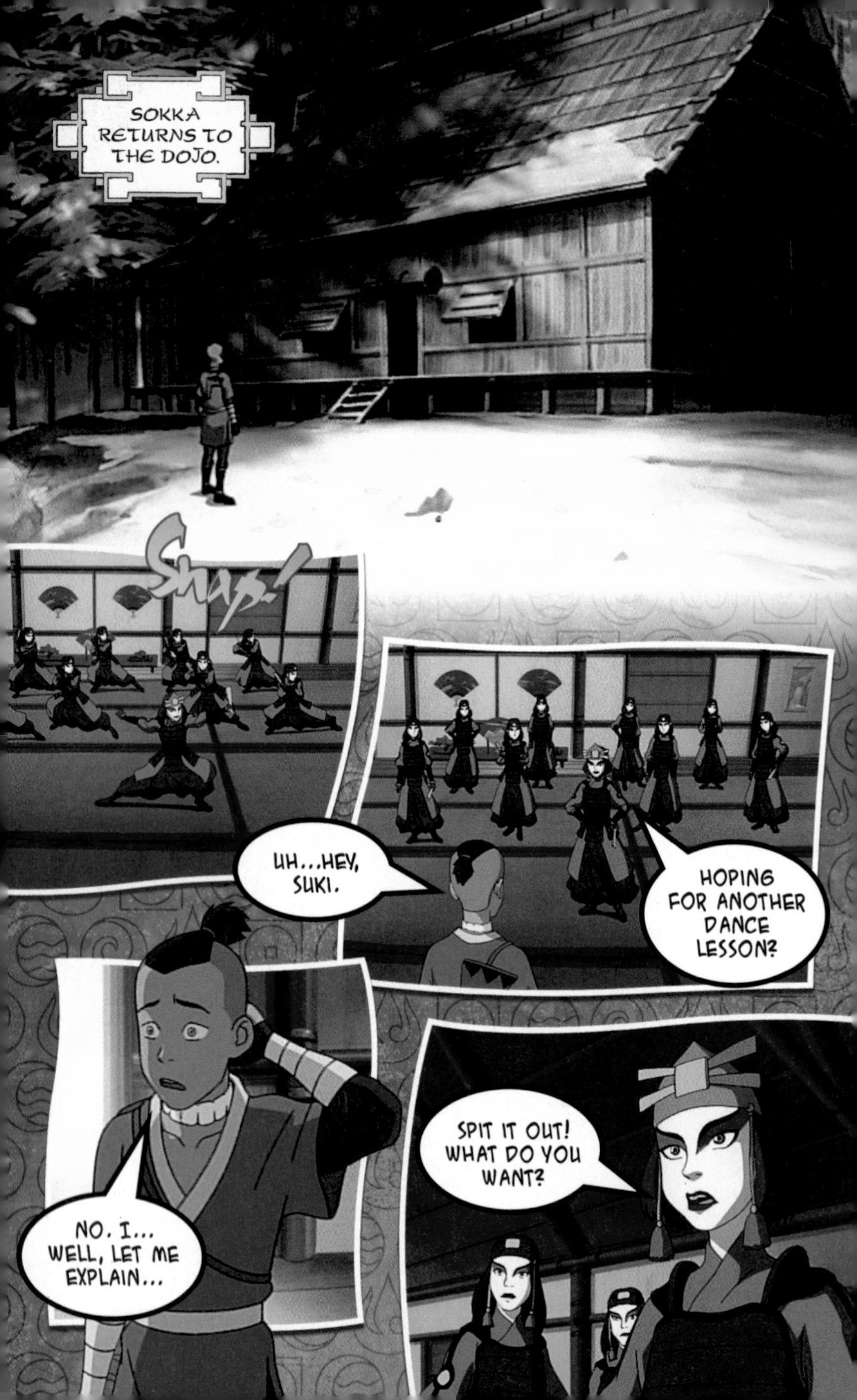
SOKKA RETURNS TO THE DOJO.
Snap!
UH...HEY, SUKI.
HOPING FOR ANOTHER DANCE LESSON?
NO. I... WELL, LET ME EXPLAIN...
SPIT IT OUT! WHAT DO YOU WANT?

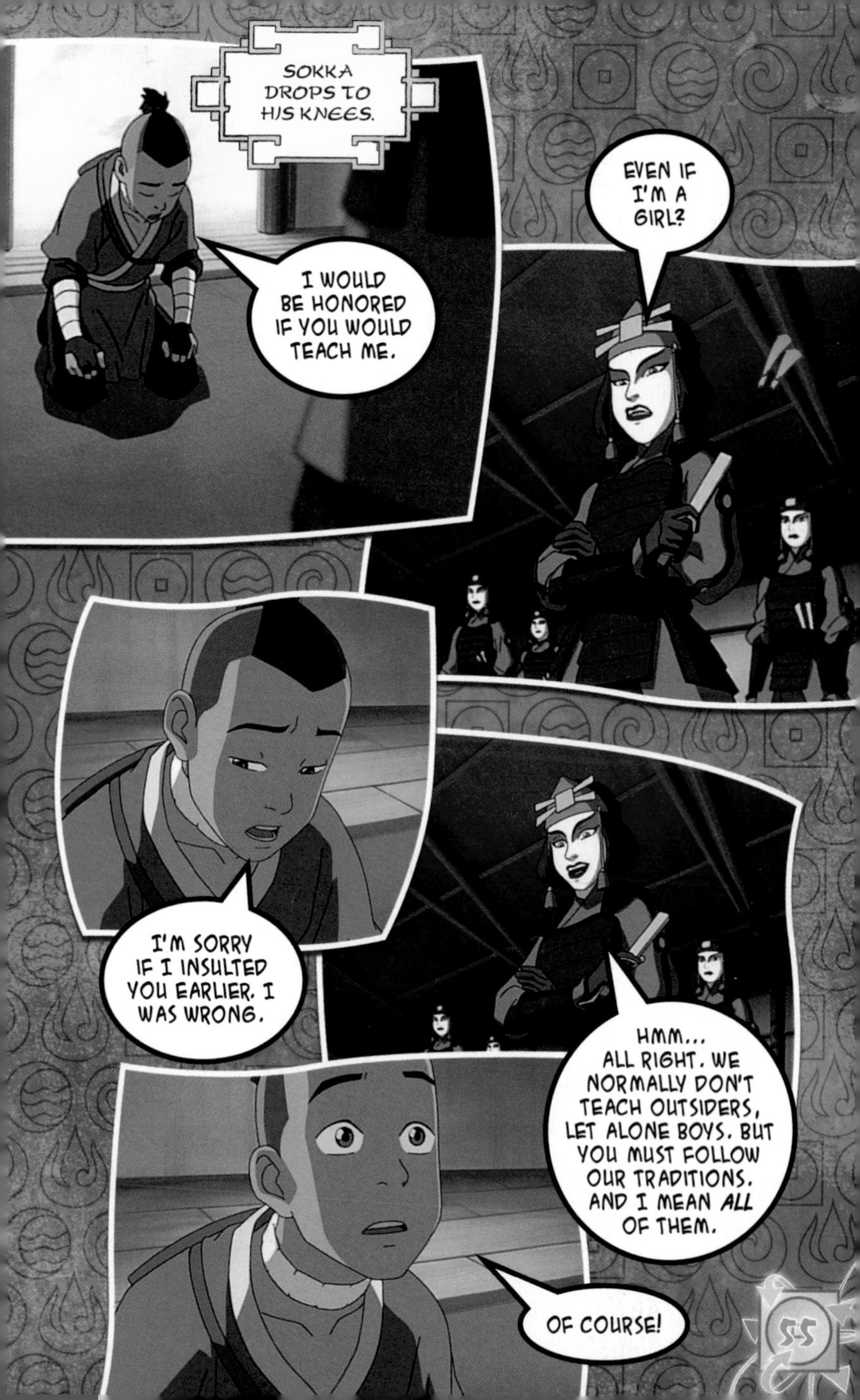

SOKKA DROPS TO HIS KNEES.
I WOULD BE HONORED IF YOU WOULD TEACH ME.
EVEN IF I'M A GIRL?
I'M SORRY IF I INSULTED YOU EARLIER. I WAS WRONG.
HMM... ALL RIGHT. WE NORMALLY DON'T TEACH OUTSIDERS, LET ALONE BOYS. BUT YOU MUST FOLLOW OUR TRADITIONS. AND I MEAN *ALL* OF THEM.
OF COURSE!

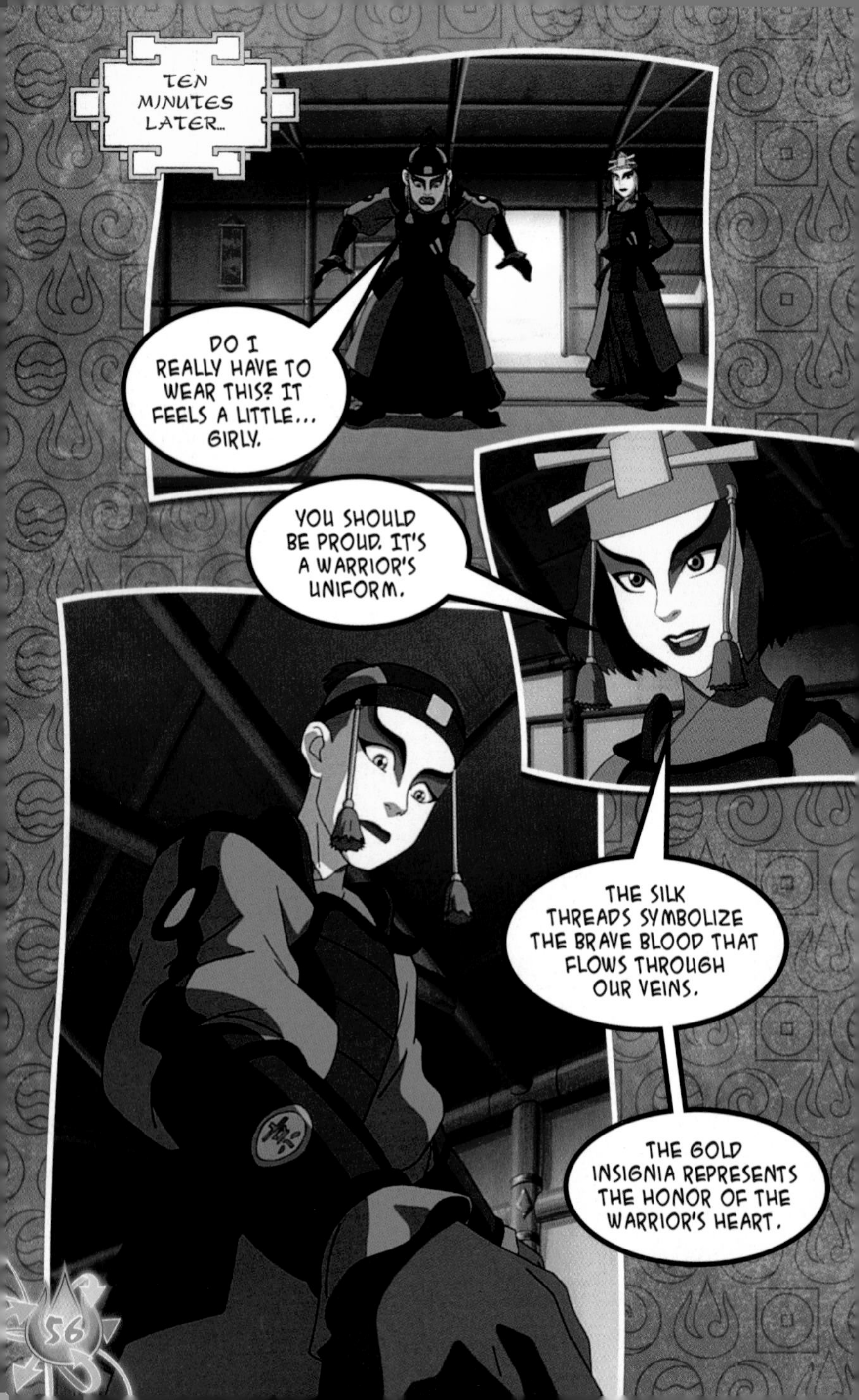
TEN MINUTES LATER...
DO I REALLY HAVE TO WEAR THIS? IT FEELS A LITTLE... GIRLY.
YOU SHOULD BE PROUD. IT'S A WARRIOR'S UNIFORM.
THE SILK THREADS SYMBOLIZE THE BRAVE BLOOD THAT FLOWS THROUGH OUR VEINS.
THE GOLD INSIGNIA REPRESENTS THE HONOR OF THE WARRIOR'S HEART.

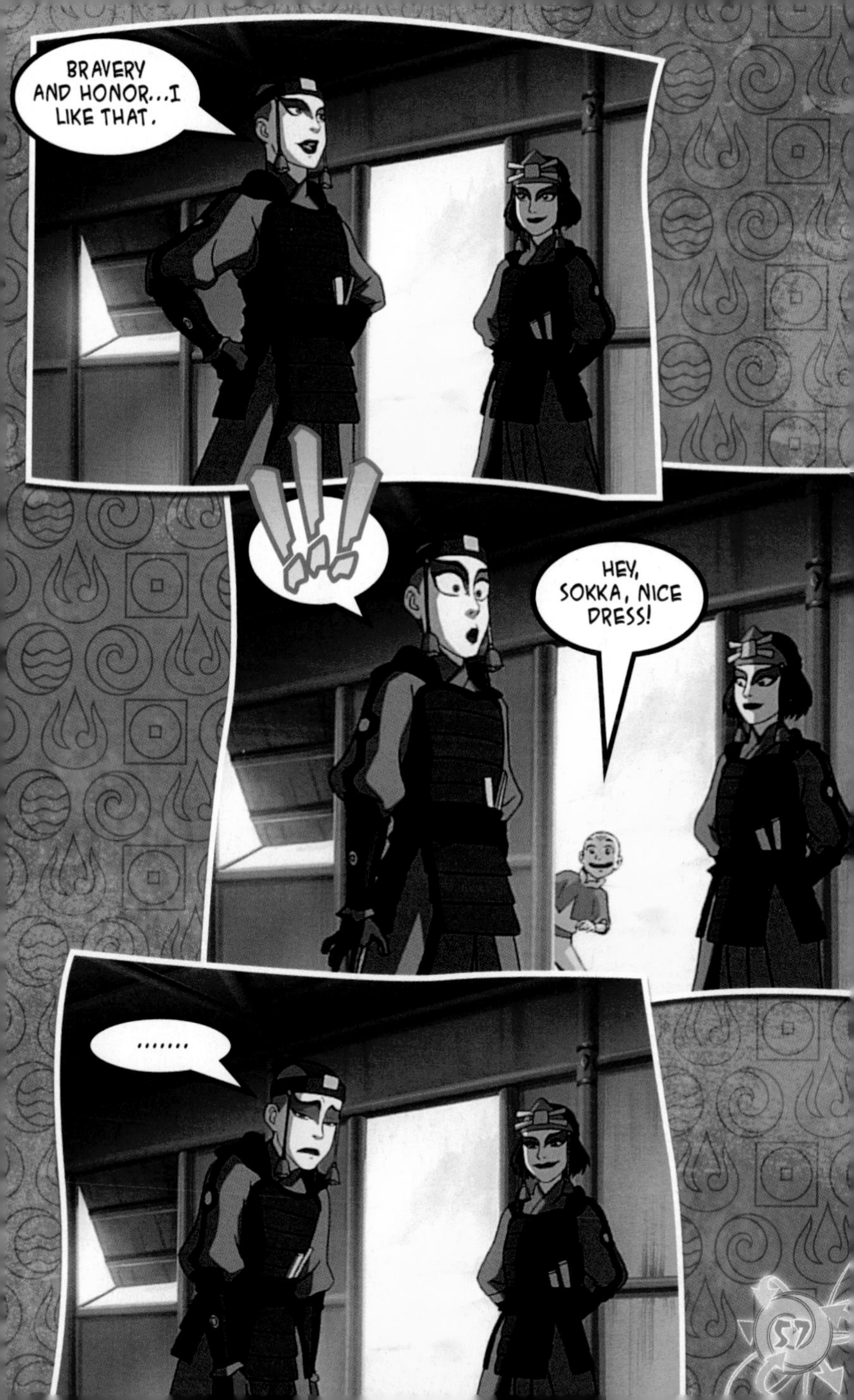
BRAVERY AND HONOR...I LIKE THAT.
!!!
HEY, SOKKA, NICE DRESS!
....

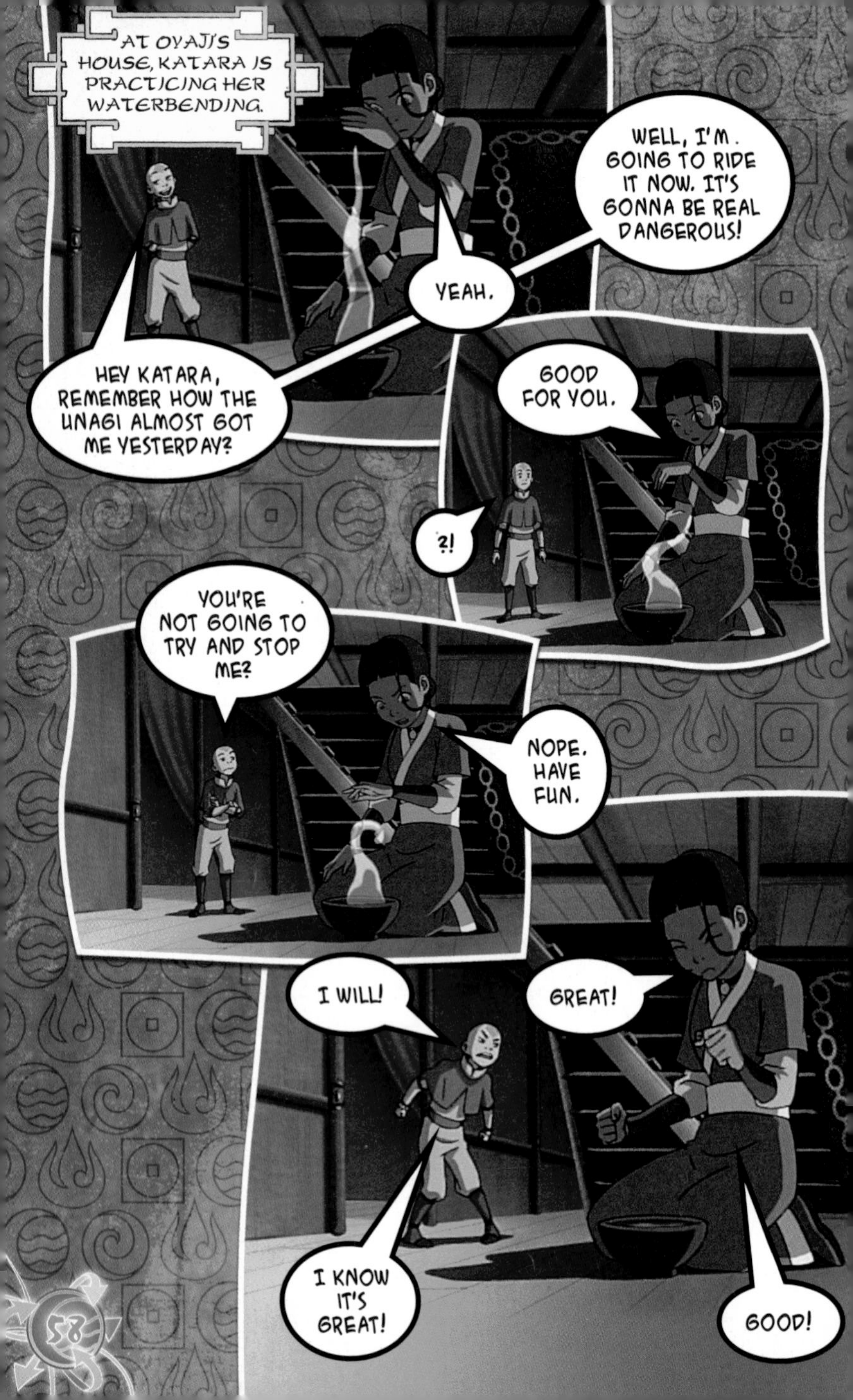
AT OYAJI'S HOUSE, KATARA IS PRACTICING HER WATERBENDING.
HEY KATARA, REMEMBER HOW THE UNAGI ALMOST GOT ME YESTERDAY?
YEAH.
WELL, I'M GOING TO RIDE IT NOW. IT'S GONNA BE REAL DANGEROUS!
GOOD FOR YOU.
?!
YOU'RE NOT GOING TO TRY AND STOP ME?
NOPE. HAVE FUN.
I WILL!
GREAT!
I KNOW IT'S GREAT!
GOOD!
58

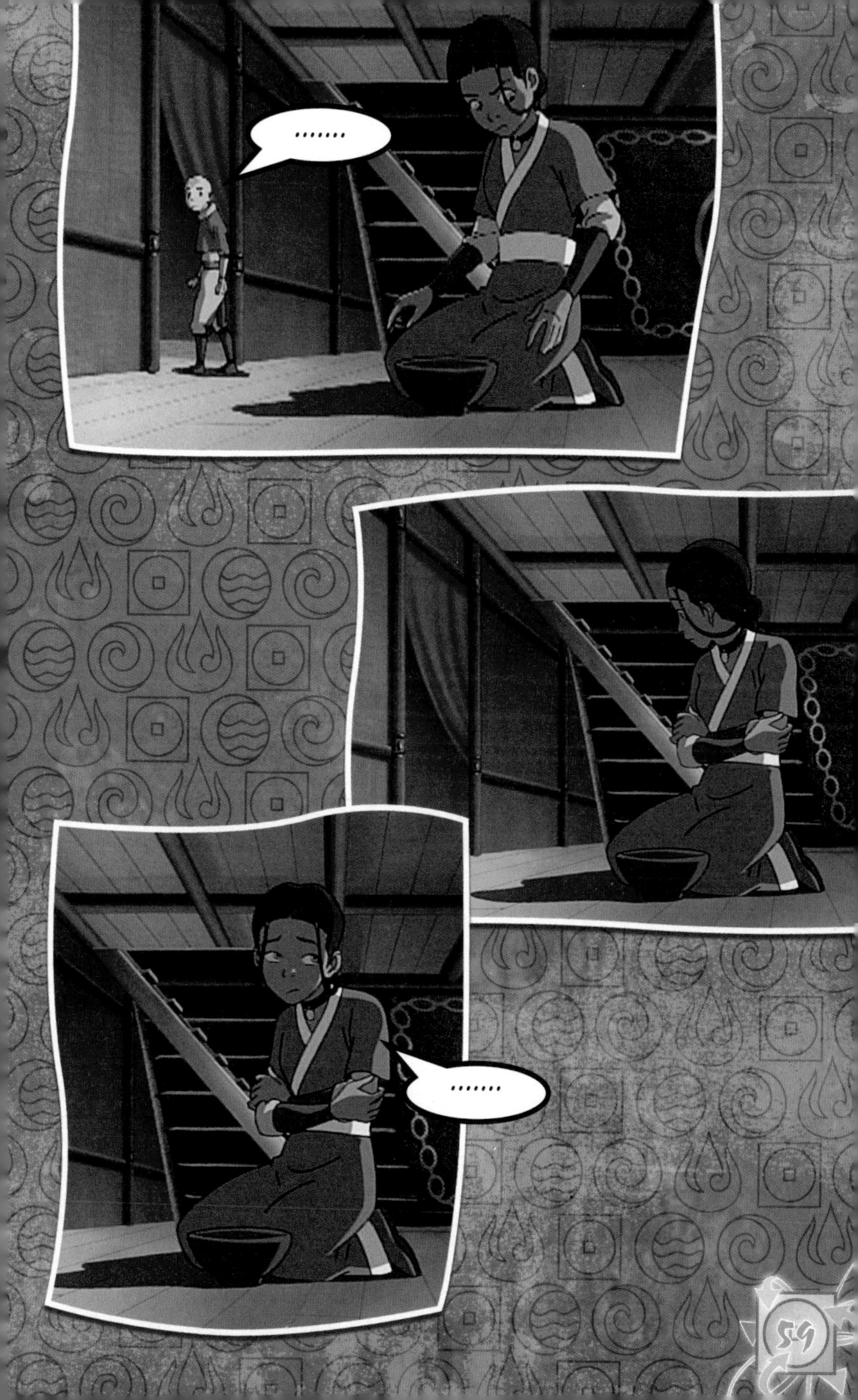

....
....

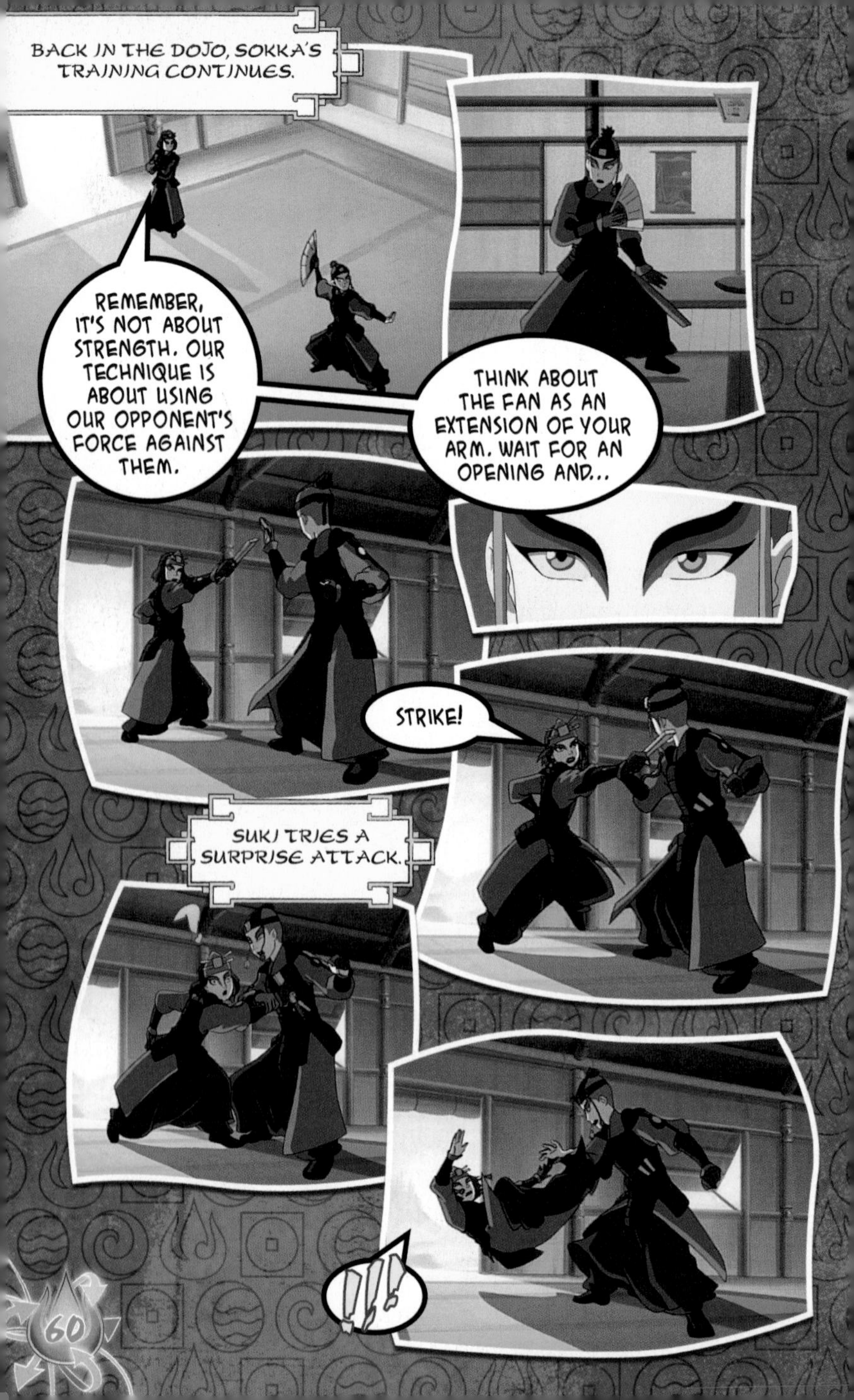

BACK IN THE DOJO, SOKKA'S TRAINING CONTINUES.
REMEMBER, IT'S NOT ABOUT STRENGTH. OUR TECHNIQUE IS ABOUT USING OUR OPPONENT'S FORCE AGAINST THEM.
THINK ABOUT THE FAN AS AN EXTENSION OF YOUR ARM. WAIT FOR AN OPENING AND...
STRIKE!
SUKI TRIES A SURPRISE ATTACK.
!!!

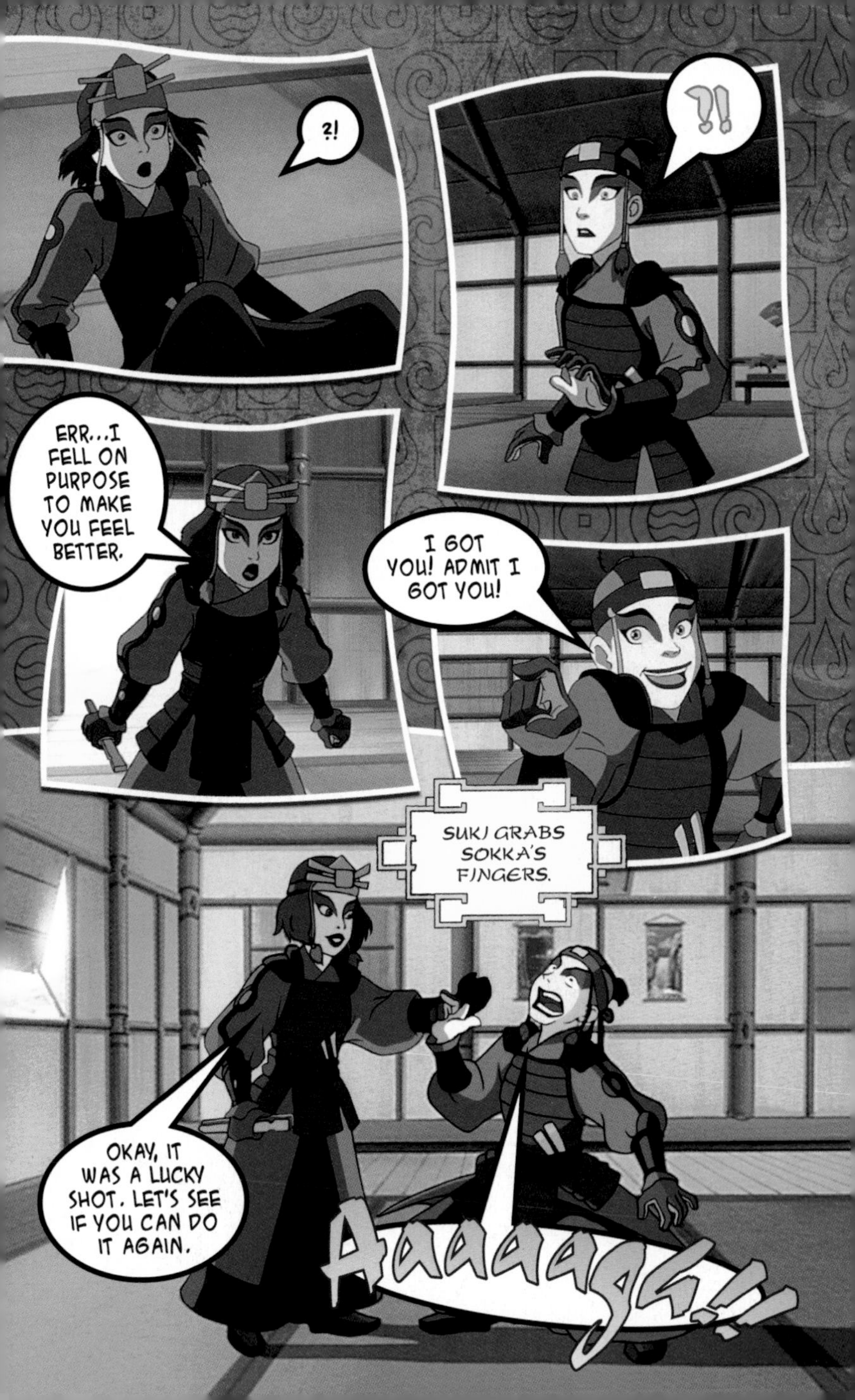
?!
?!
ERR...I FELL ON PURPOSE TO MAKE YOU FEEL BETTER.
I GOT YOU! ADMIT I GOT YOU!
SUKI GRABS SOKKA'S FINGERS.
OKAY, IT WAS A LUCKY SHOT. LET'S SEE IF YOU CAN DO IT AGAIN.
Aaaaagh!!

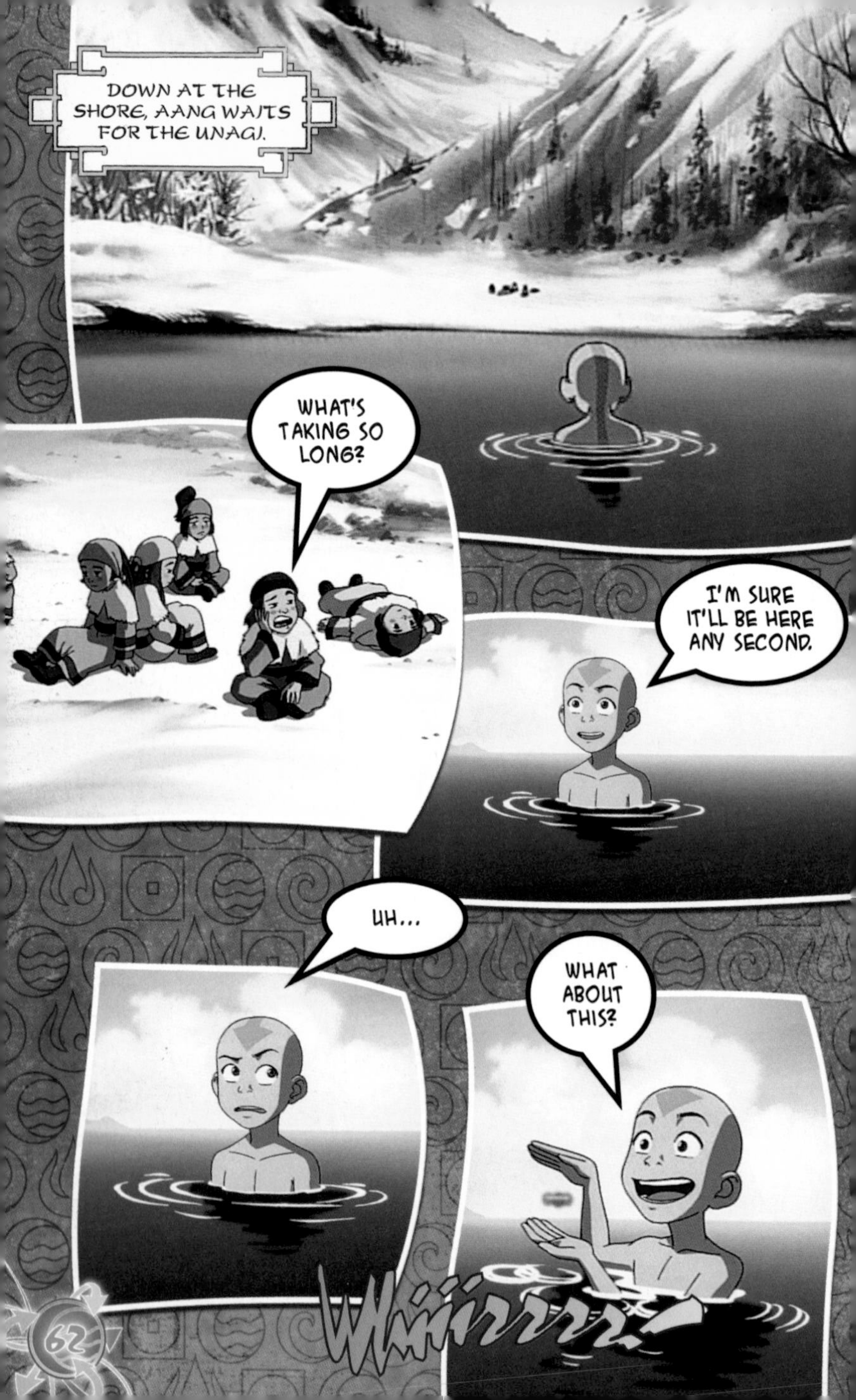
DOWN AT THE SHORE, AANG WAITS FOR THE UNAGI.
WHAT'S TAKING SO LONG?
I'M SURE IT'LL BE HERE ANY SECOND.
UH...
WHAT ABOUT THIS?
Whiiirrrrr!

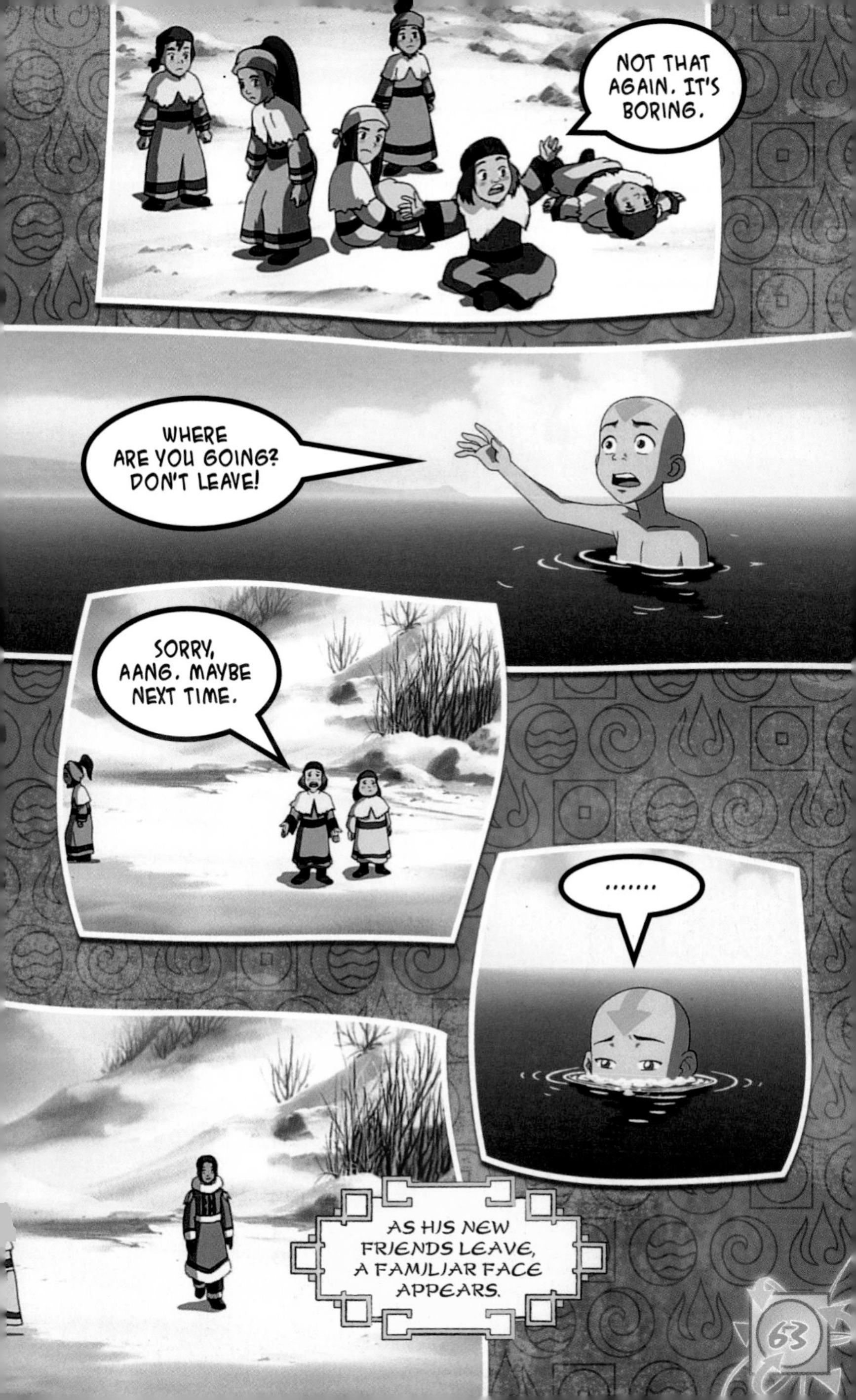
NOT THAT AGAIN. IT'S BORING.
WHERE ARE YOU GOING? DON'T LEAVE!
SORRY, AANG. MAYBE NEXT TIME.
....
AS HIS NEW FRIENDS LEAVE, A FAMILIAR FACE APPEARS.

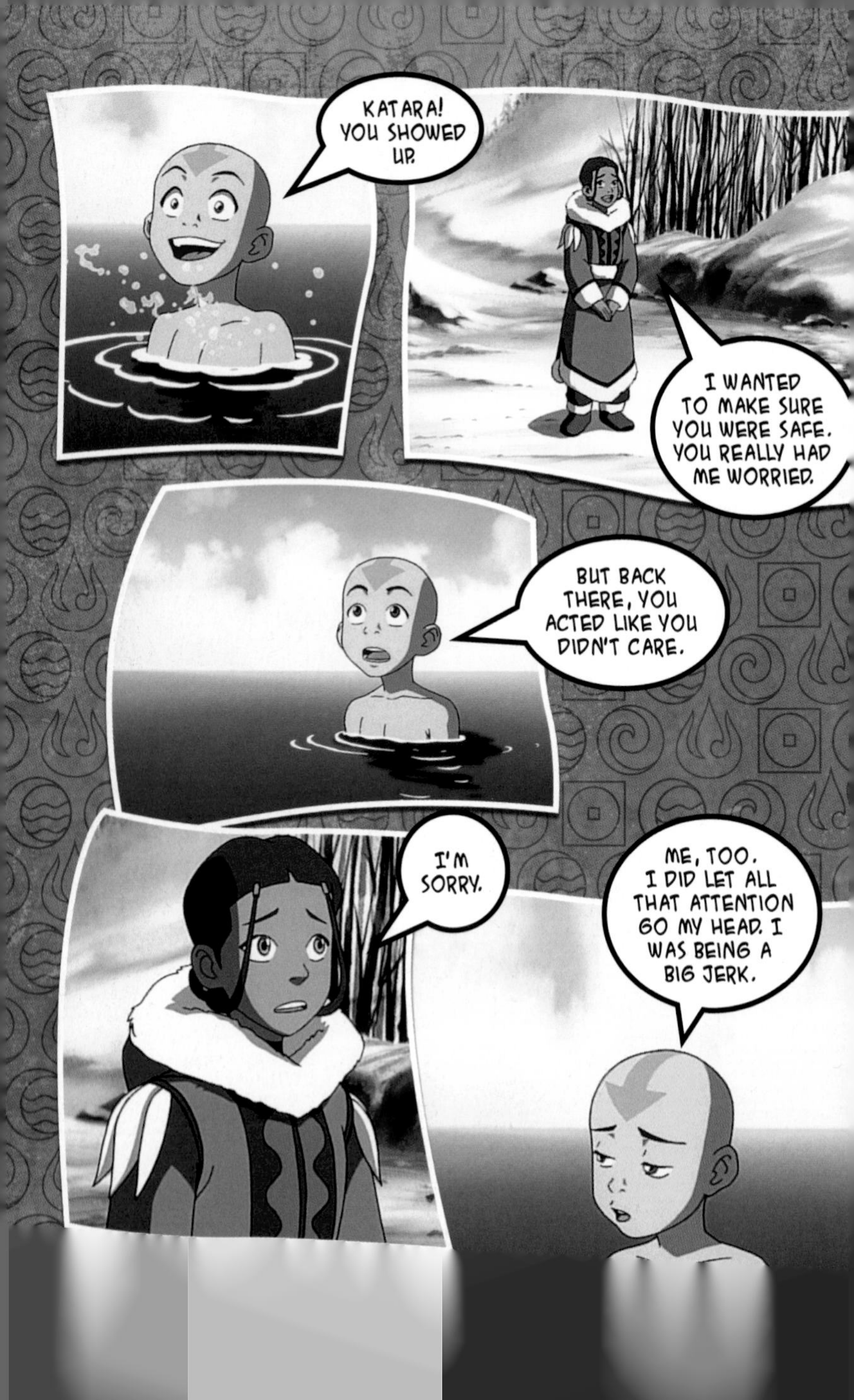
KATARA! YOU SHOWED UP.
I WANTED TO MAKE SURE YOU WERE SAFE. YOU REALLY HAD ME WORRIED.
BUT BACK THERE, YOU ACTED LIKE YOU DIDN'T CARE.
I'M SORRY.
ME, TOO. I DID LET ALL THAT ATTENTION GO MY HEAD. I WAS BEING A BIG JERK.

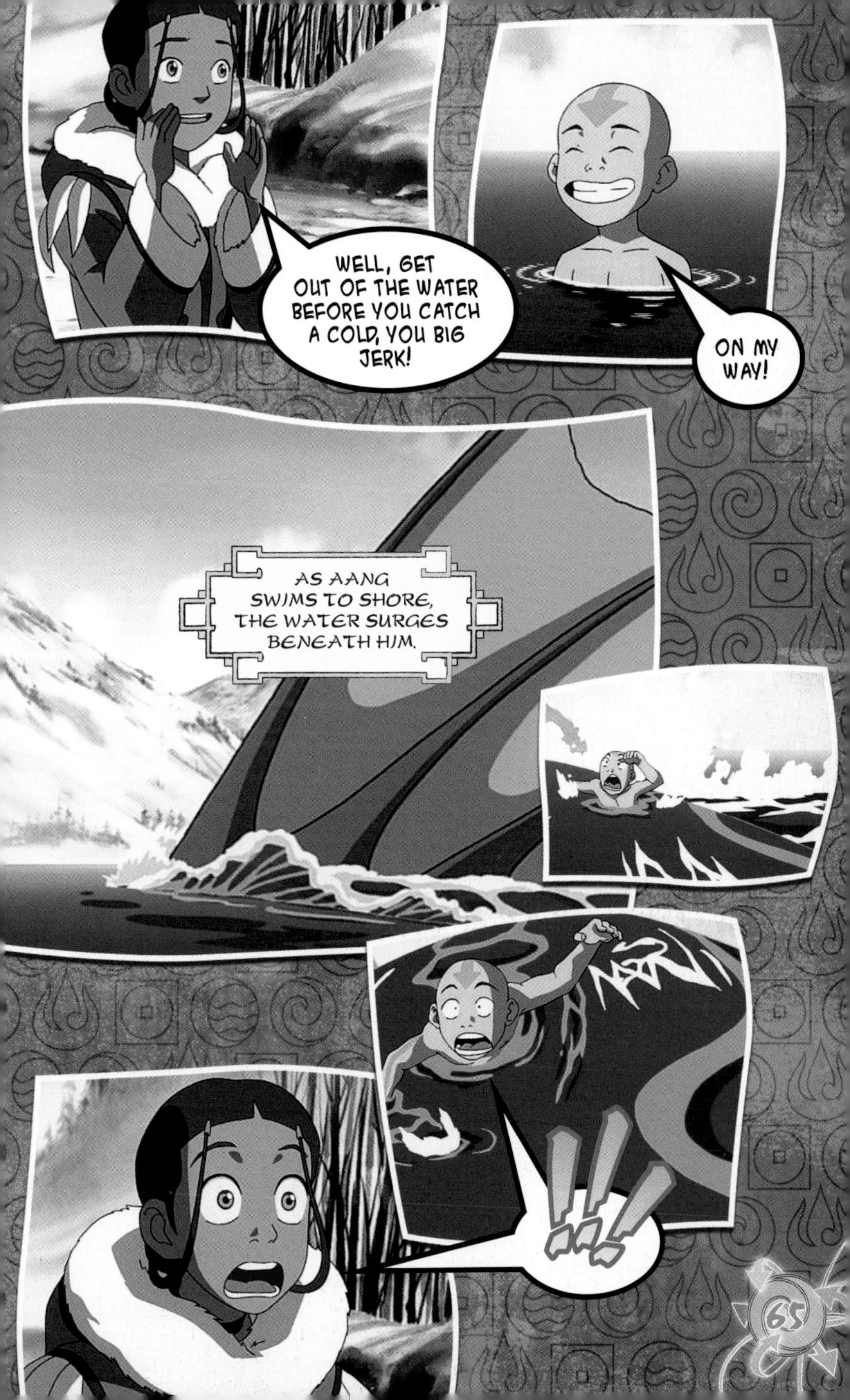
WELL, GET OUT OF THE WATER BEFORE YOU CATCH A COLD, YOU BIG JERK!
ON MY WAY!
AS AANG SWIMS TO SHORE, THE WATER SURGES BENEATH HIM.
65

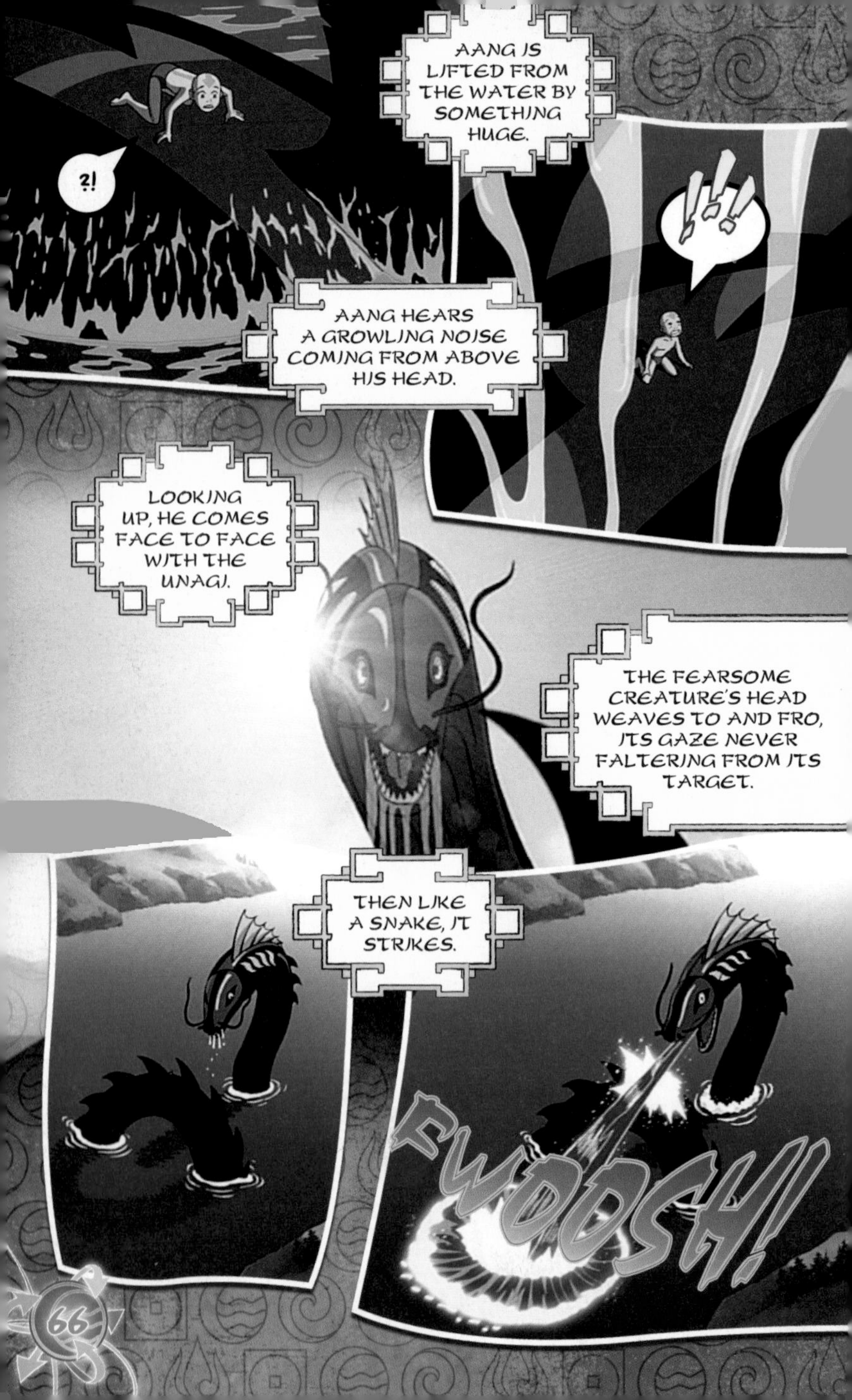

AANG IS LIFTED FROM THE WATER BY SOMETHING HUGE.
?!
!!!
AANG HEARS A GROWLING NOISE COMING FROM ABOVE HIS HEAD.
LOOKING UP, HE COMES FACE TO FACE WITH THE UNAGI.
THE FEARSOME CREATURE'S HEAD WEAVES TO AND FRO, ITS GAZE NEVER FALTERING FROM ITS TARGET.
THEN LIKE A SNAKE, IT STRIKES.
FWOOSH!

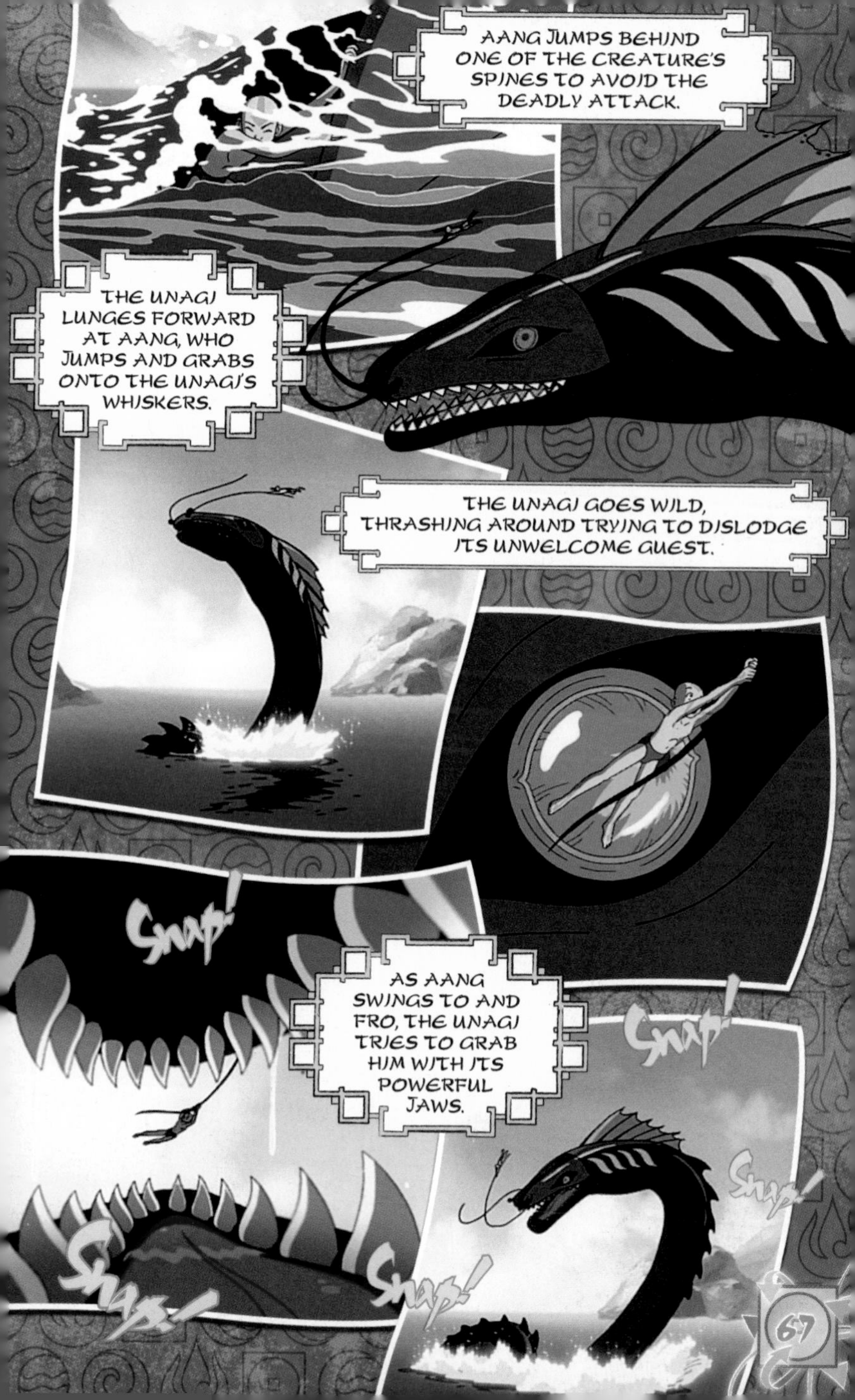
AANG JUMPS BEHIND ONE OF THE CREATURE'S SPINES TO AVOID THE DEADLY ATTACK.
THE UNAGI LUNGES FORWARD AT AANG, WHO JUMPS AND GRABS ONTO THE UNAGI'S WHISKERS.
THE UNAGI GOES WILD, THRASHING AROUND TRYING TO DISLODGE ITS UNWELCOME GUEST.
Snap!
AS AANG SWINGS TO AND FRO, THE UNAGI TRIES TO GRAB HIM WITH ITS POWERFUL JAWS.
Snap!
Snap!
Snap!
Snap!

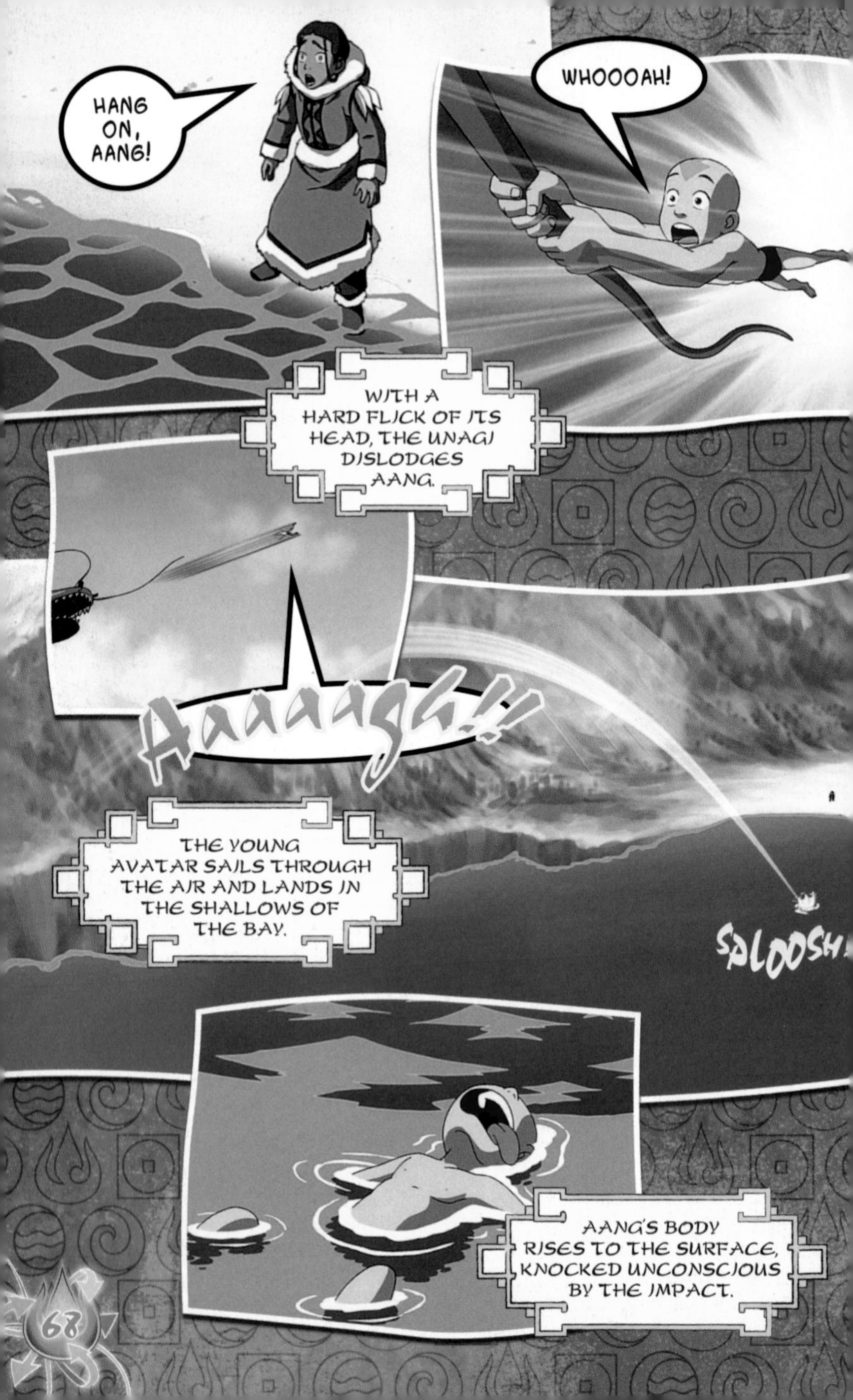
HANG ON, AANG!
WHOOOAH!
WITH A HARD FLICK OF ITS HEAD, THE UNAGI DISLODGES AANG.
Aaaaagh!!
THE YOUNG AVATAR SAILS THROUGH THE AIR AND LANDS IN THE SHALLOWS OF THE BAY.
SPLOOSH!
AANG'S BODY RISES TO THE SURFACE, KNOCKED UNCONSCIOUS BY THE IMPACT.

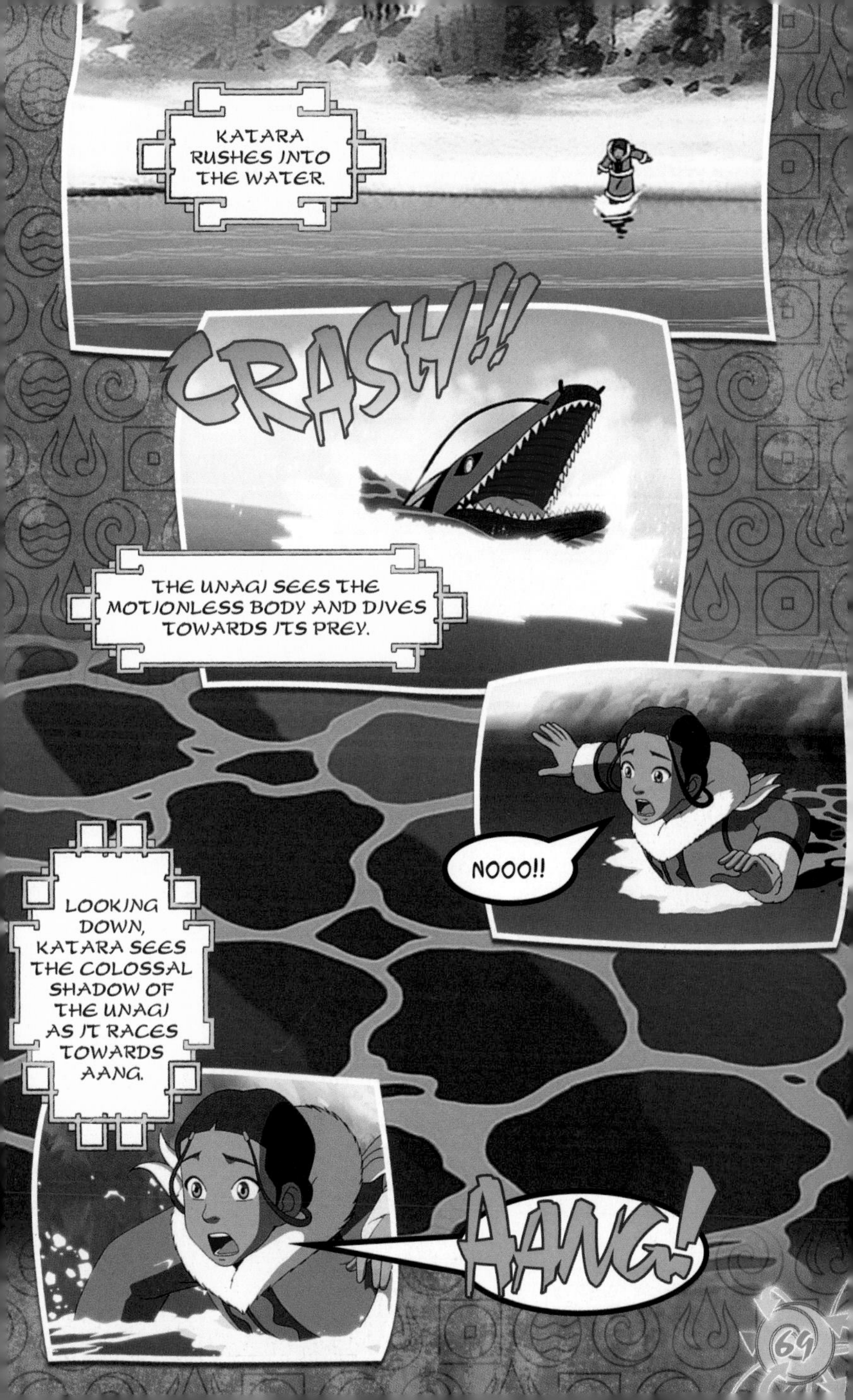

KATARA RUSHES INTO THE WATER.
CRASH!!
THE UNAGI SEES THE MOTIONLESS BODY AND DIVES TOWARDS ITS PREY.
NOOO!!
LOOKING DOWN, KATARA SEES THE COLOSSAL SHADOW OF THE UNAGI AS IT RACES TOWARDS AANG.
AANG!

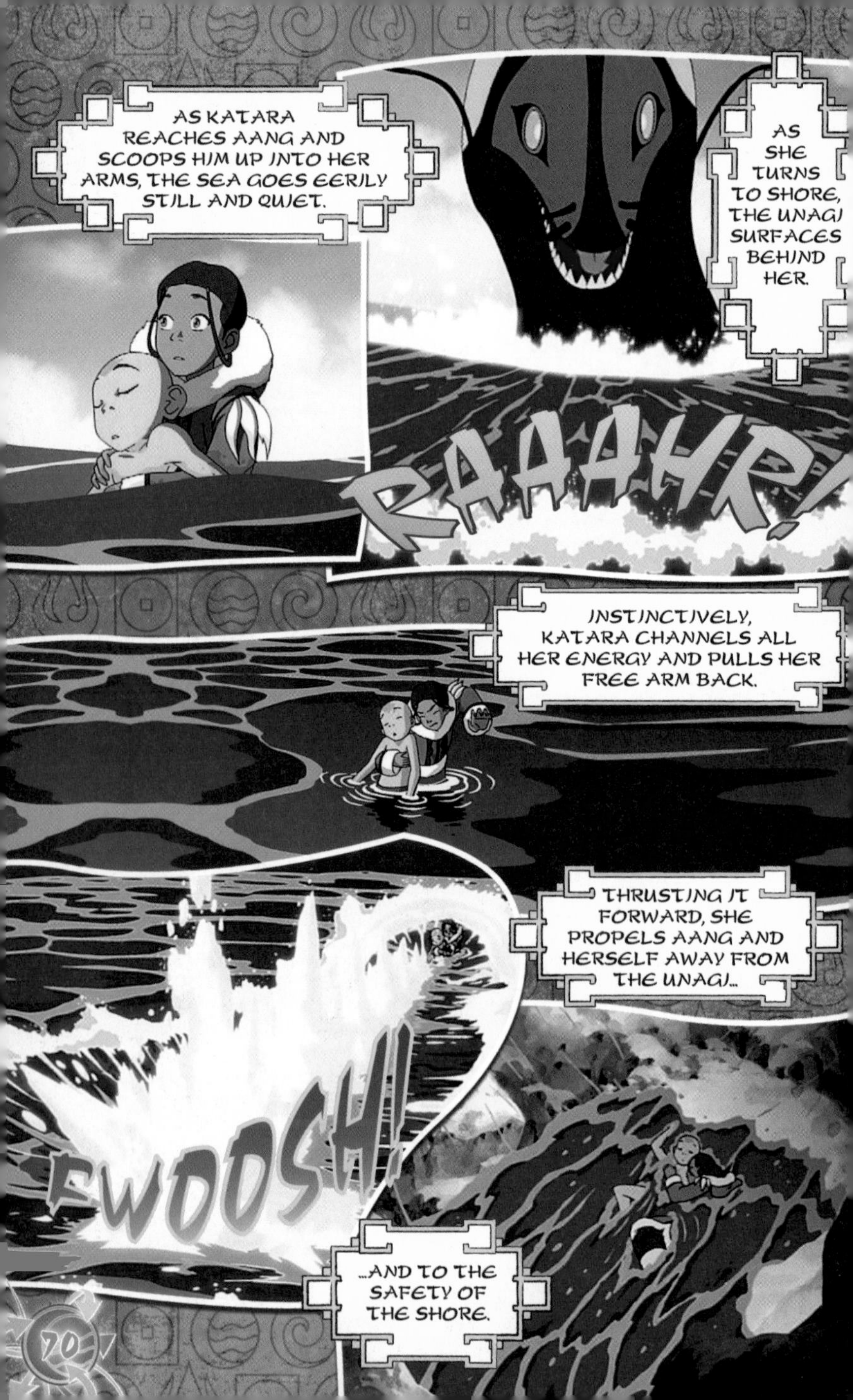
AS KATARA REACHES AANG AND SCOOPS HIM UP INTO HER ARMS, THE SEA GOES EERILY STILL AND QUIET.
AS SHE TURNS TO SHORE, THE UNAGI SURFACES BEHIND HER.
RAAAHR!
INSTINCTIVELY, KATARA CHANNELS ALL HER ENERGY AND PULLS HER FREE ARM BACK.
THRUSTING IT FORWARD, SHE PROPELS AANG AND HERSELF AWAY FROM THE UNAGI...
FWOOSH!
...AND TO THE SAFETY OF THE SHORE.

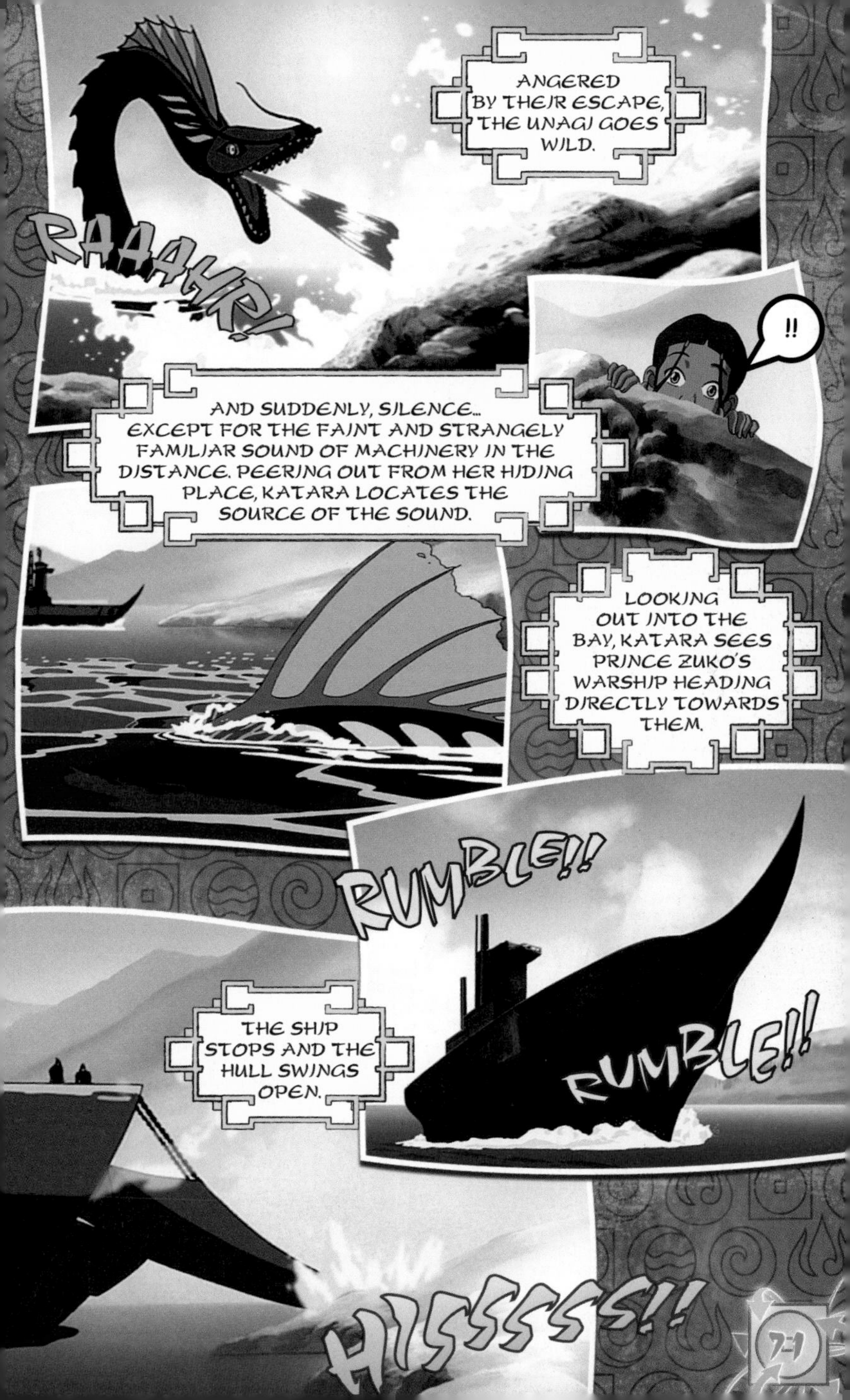

ANGERED BY THEIR ESCAPE, THE UNAGI GOES WILD.
RAAAAHR!!
!!
AND SUDDENLY, SILENCE... EXCEPT FOR THE FAINT AND STRANGELY FAMILIAR SOUND OF MACHINERY IN THE DISTANCE. PEERING OUT FROM HER HIDING PLACE, KATARA LOCATES THE SOURCE OF THE SOUND.
LOOKING OUT INTO THE BAY, KATARA SEES PRINCE ZUKO'S WARSHIP HEADING DIRECTLY TOWARDS THEM.
RUMBLE!!
RUMBLE!!
THE SHIP STOPS AND THE HULL SWINGS OPEN.
HISSSSS!!

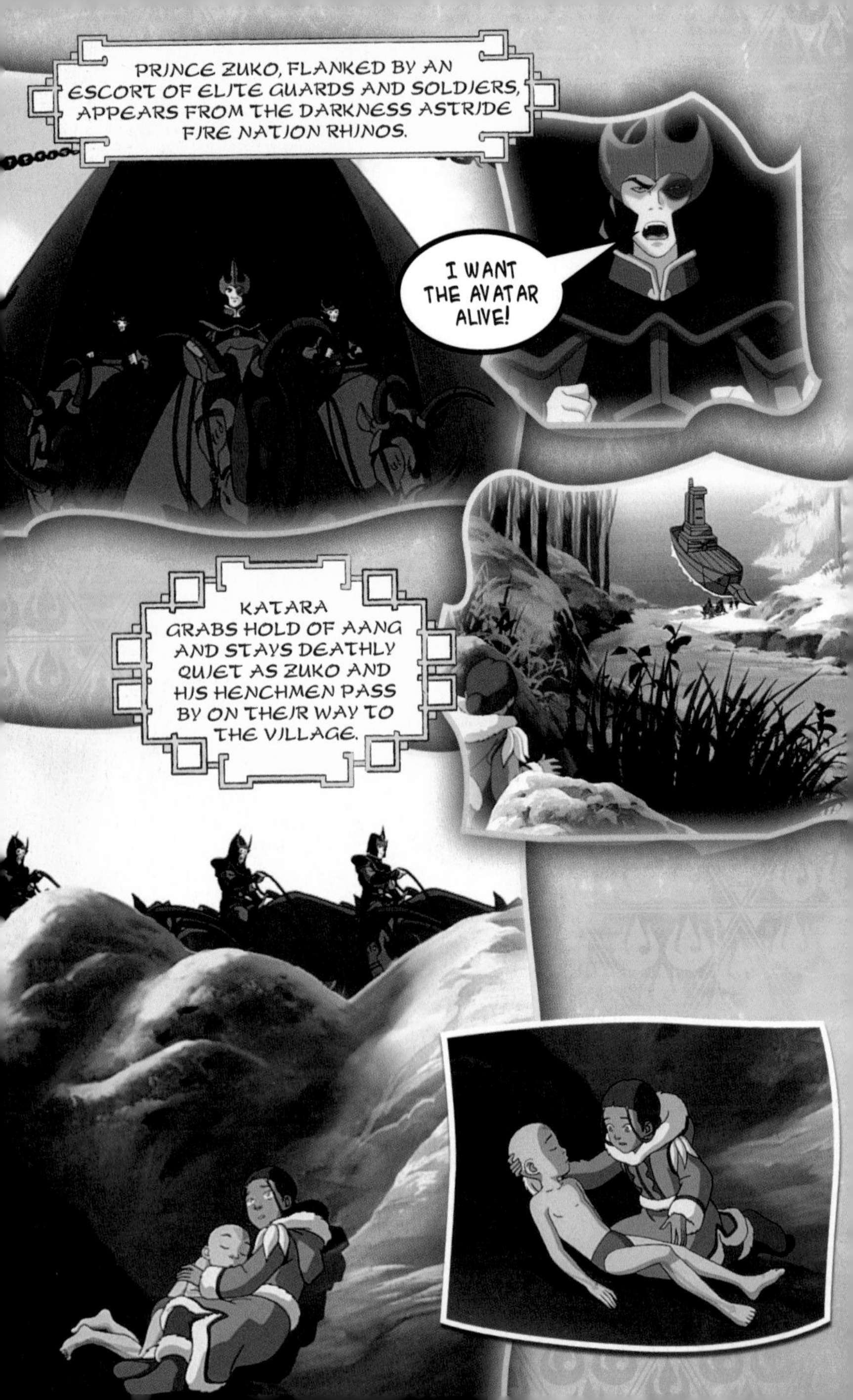
PRINCE ZUKO, FLANKED BY AN ESCORT OF ELITE GUARDS AND SOLDIERS, APPEARS FROM THE DARKNESS ASTRIDE FIRE NATION RHINOS.
I WANT THE AVATAR ALIVE!
KATARA GRABS HOLD OF AANG AND STAYS DEATHLY QUIET AS ZUKO AND HIS HENCHMEN PASS BY ON THEIR WAY TO THE VILLAGE.

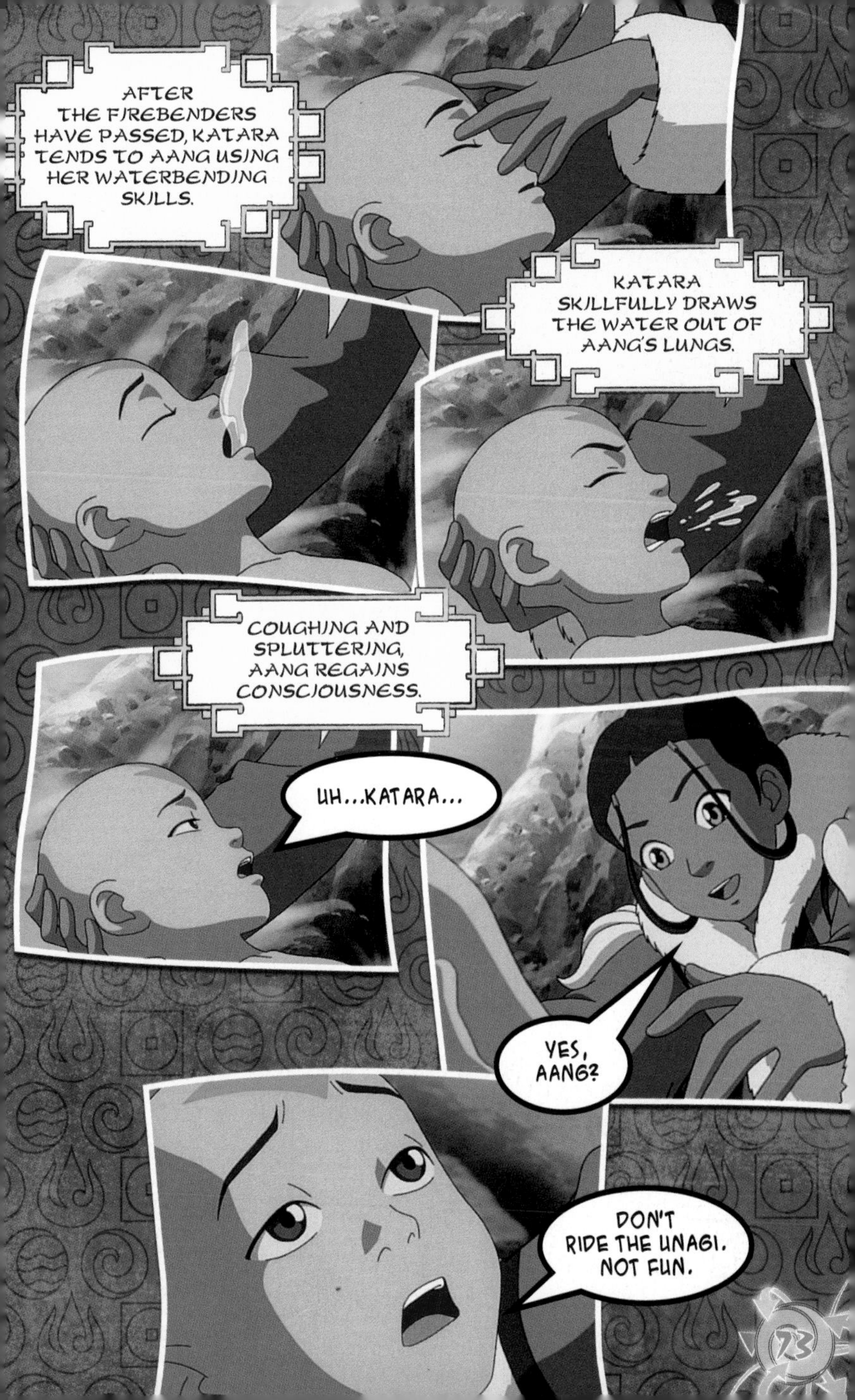
AFTER THE FIREBENDERS HAVE PASSED, KATARA TENDS TO AANG USING HER WATERBENDING SKILLS.
KATARA SKILLFULLY DRAWS THE WATER OUT OF AANG'S LUNGS.
COUGHING AND SPLUTTERING, AANG REGAINS CONSCIOUSNESS.
UH...KATARA...
YES, AANG?
DON'T RIDE THE UNAGI. NOT FUN.

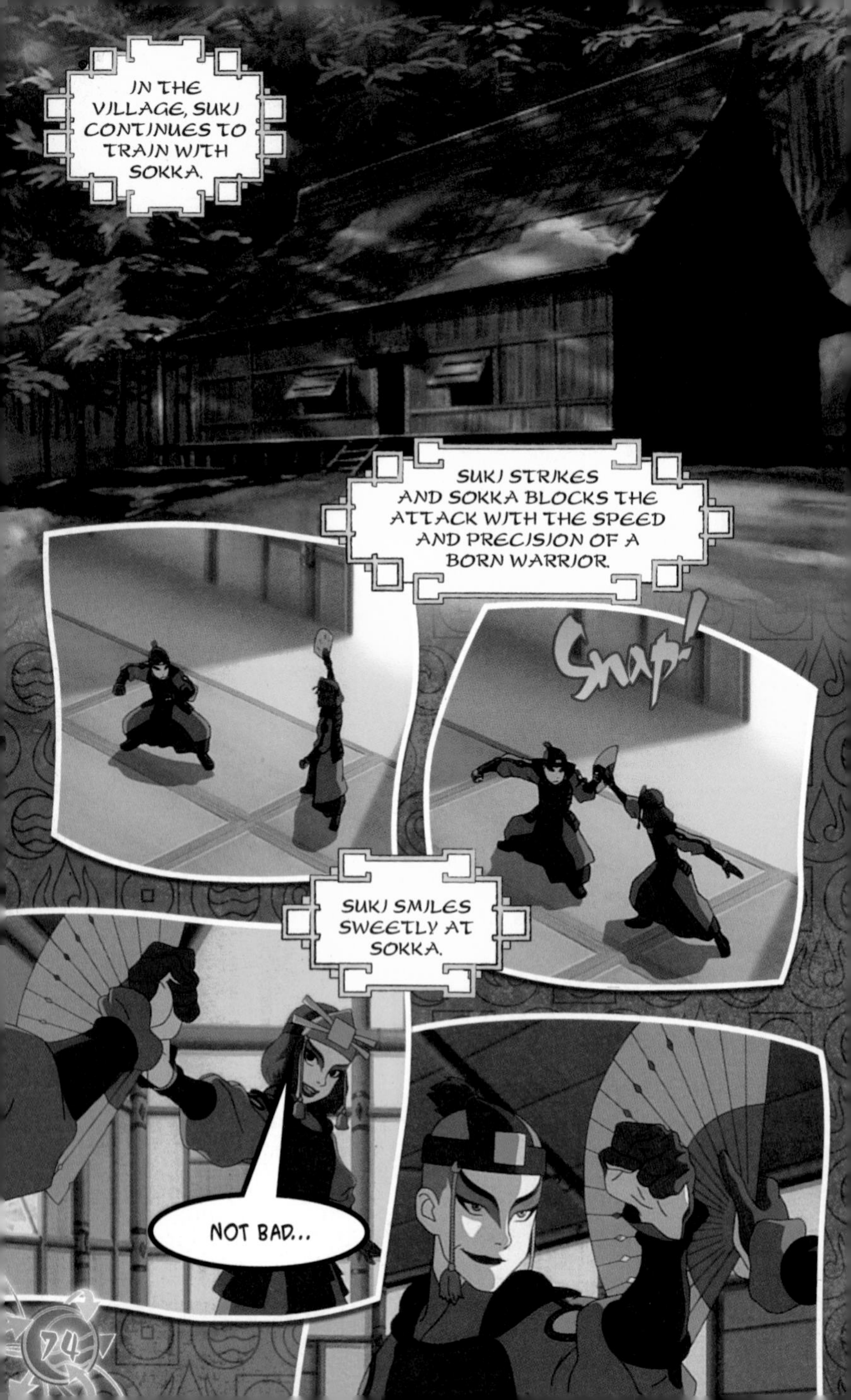
IN THE VILLAGE, SUKI CONTINUES TO TRAIN WITH SOKKA.
SUKI STRIKES AND SOKKA BLOCKS THE ATTACK WITH THE SPEED AND PRECISION OF A BORN WARRIOR.
SNAP!
SUKI SMILES SWEETLY AT SOKKA.
NOT BAD...

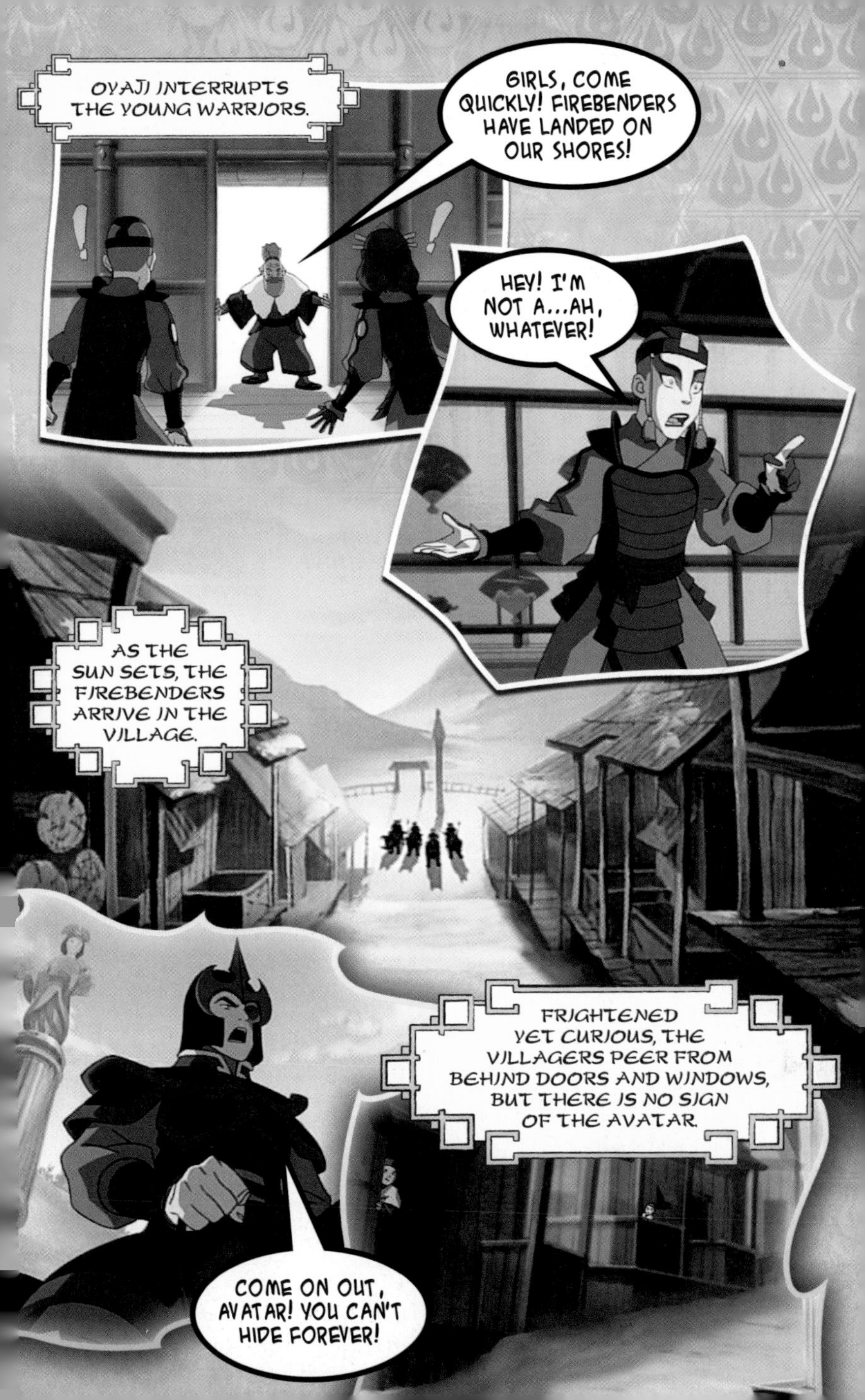

OYAJI INTERRUPTS THE YOUNG WARRIORS.
GIRLS, COME QUICKLY! FIREBENDERS HAVE LANDED ON OUR SHORES!
HEY! I'M NOT A...AH, WHATEVER!
AS THE SUN SETS, THE FIREBENDERS ARRIVE IN THE VILLAGE.
FRIGHTENED YET CURIOUS, THE VILLAGERS PEER FROM BEHIND DOORS AND WINDOWS, BUT THERE IS NO SIGN OF THE AVATAR.
COME ON OUT, AVATAR! YOU CAN'T HIDE FOREVER!

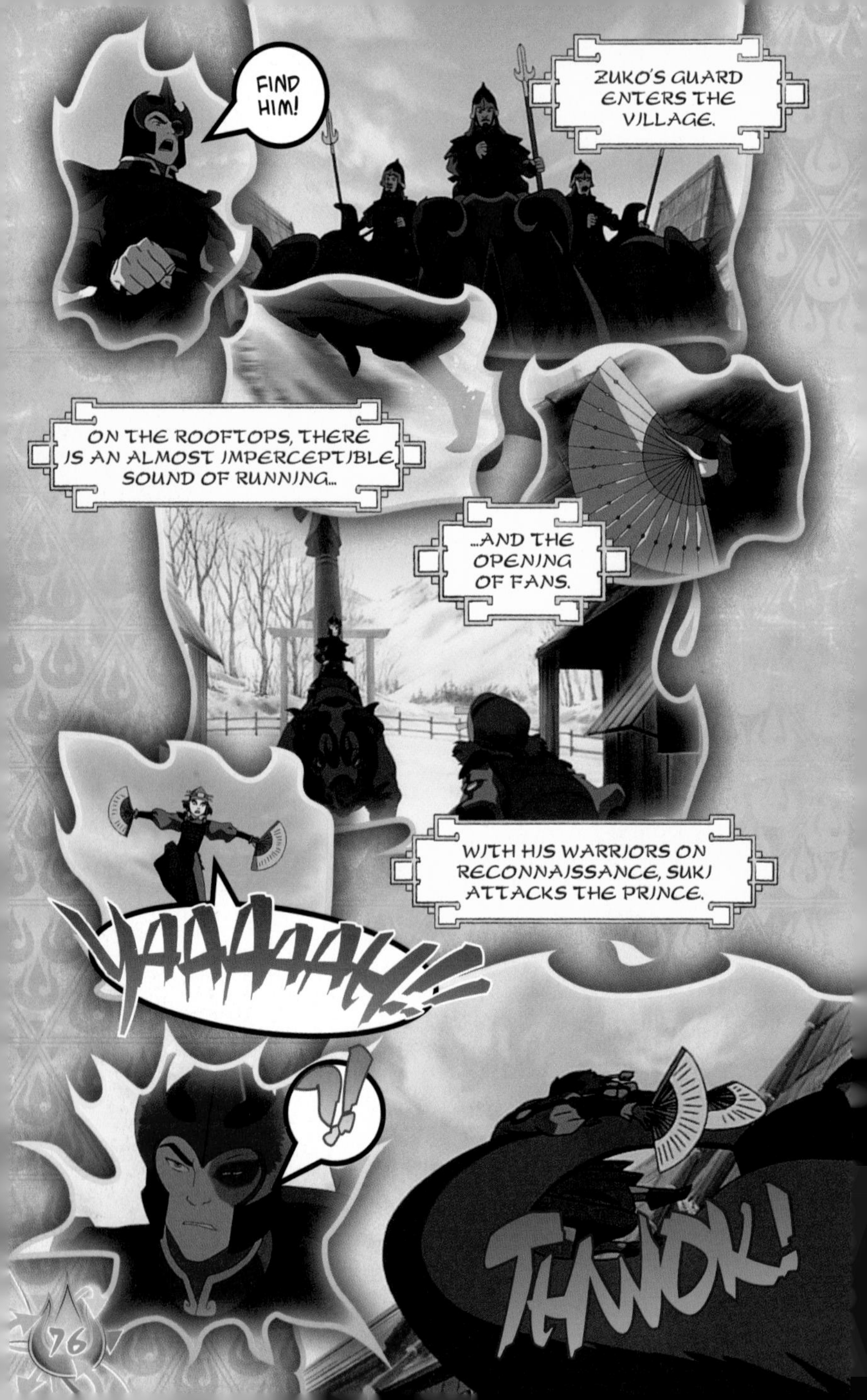
FIND HIM!
ZUKO'S GUARD ENTERS THE VILLAGE.
ON THE ROOFTOPS, THERE IS AN ALMOST IMPERCEPTIBLE SOUND OF RUNNING...
...AND THE OPENING OF FANS.
WITH HIS WARRIORS ON RECONNAISSANCE, SUKI ATTACKS THE PRINCE.
YAAAAAH!!
!
THWOK!

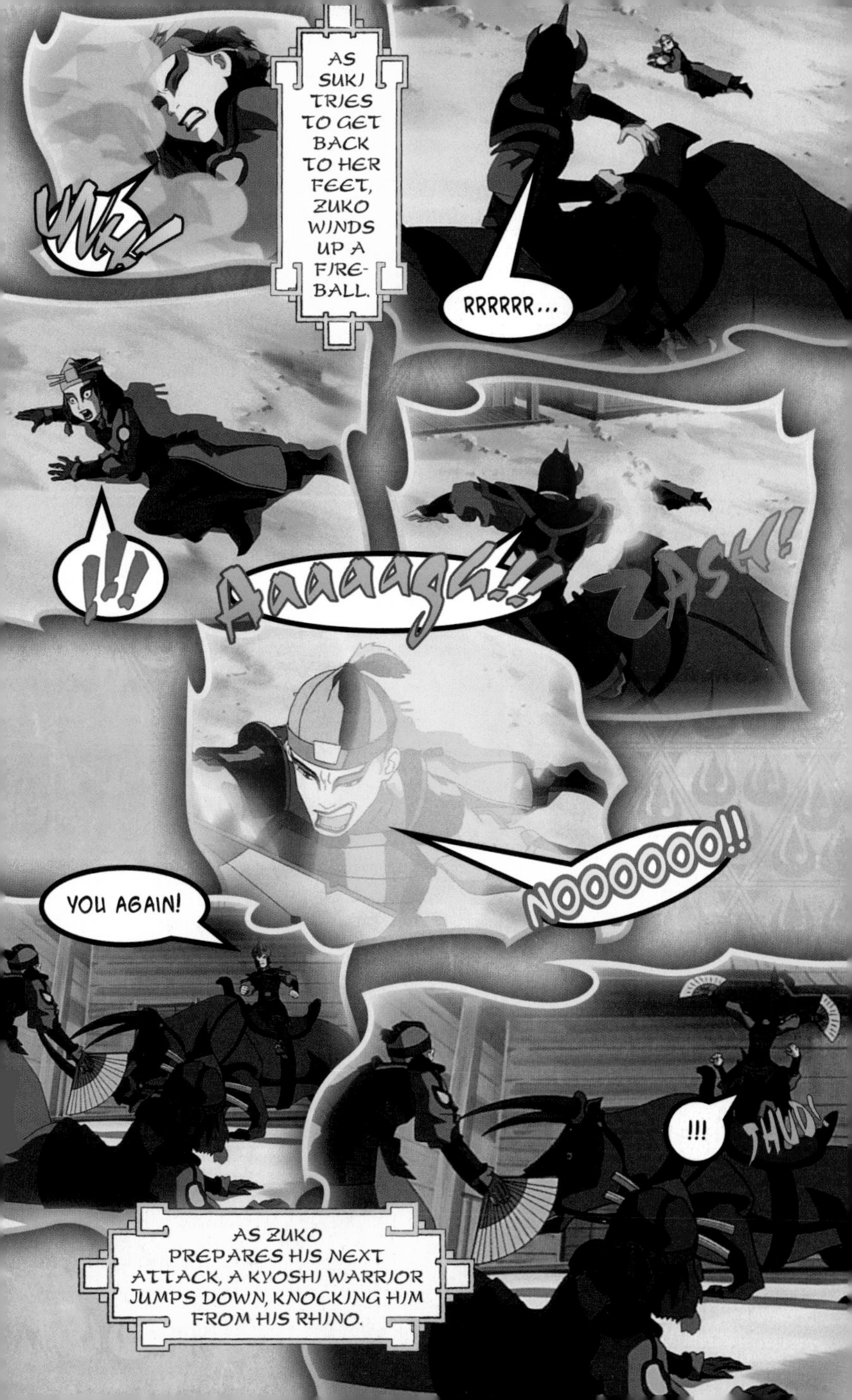
UNK!
AS SUKI TRIES TO GET BACK TO HER FEET, ZUKO WINDS UP A FIRE-BALL.
RRRRRR...
!!!
Aaaaagh!!!
ZASH!
NOOOOOO!!
YOU AGAIN!
!!!
THUD!
AS ZUKO PREPARES HIS NEXT ATTACK, A KYOSHI WARRIOR JUMPS DOWN, KNOCKING HIM FROM HIS RHINO.

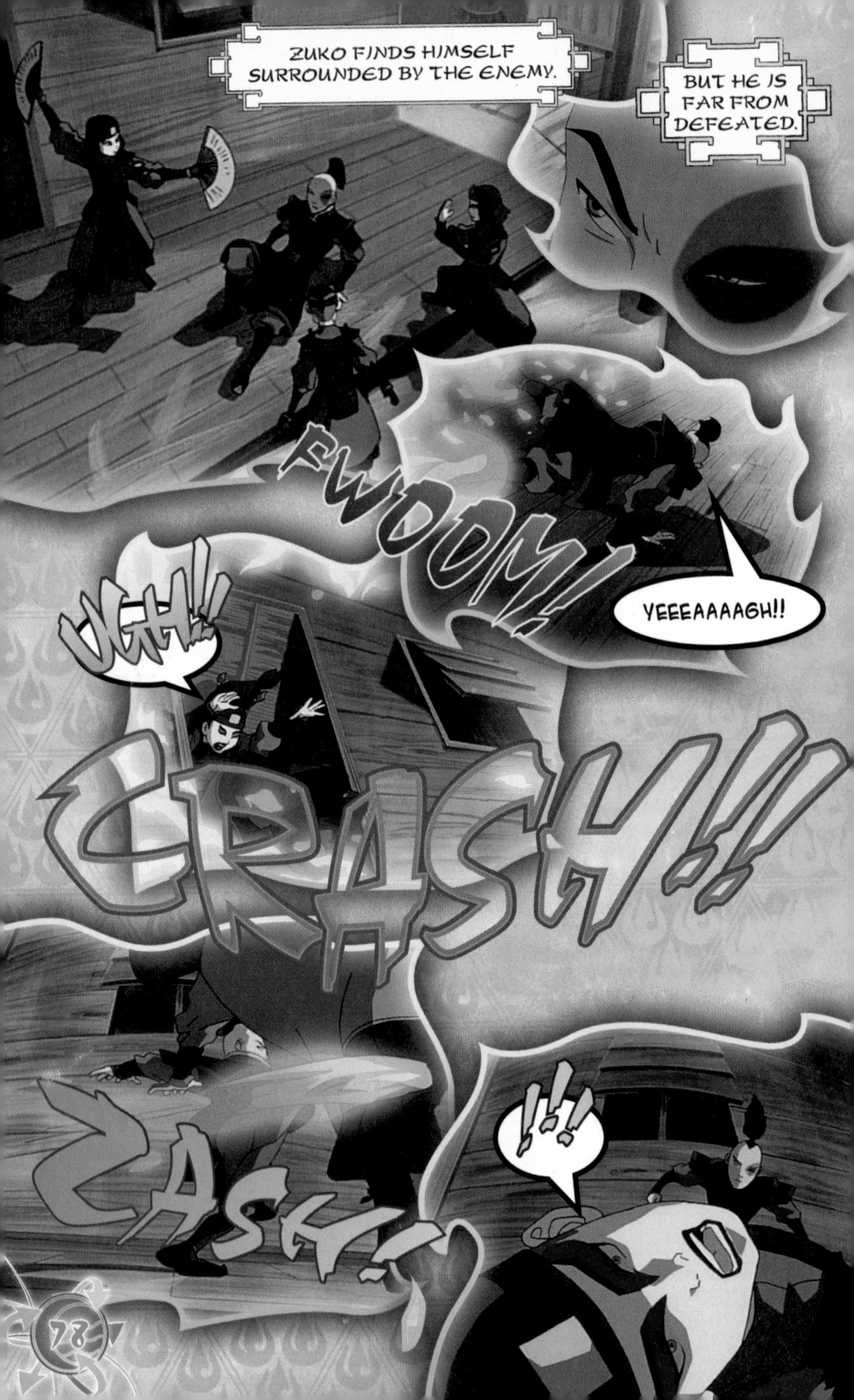
ZUKO FINDS HIMSELF SURROUNDED BY THE ENEMY.
BUT HE IS FAR FROM DEFEATED.
FWOOM!!
YEEEAAAAGH!!
UGH!!
CRASH!!
!!!

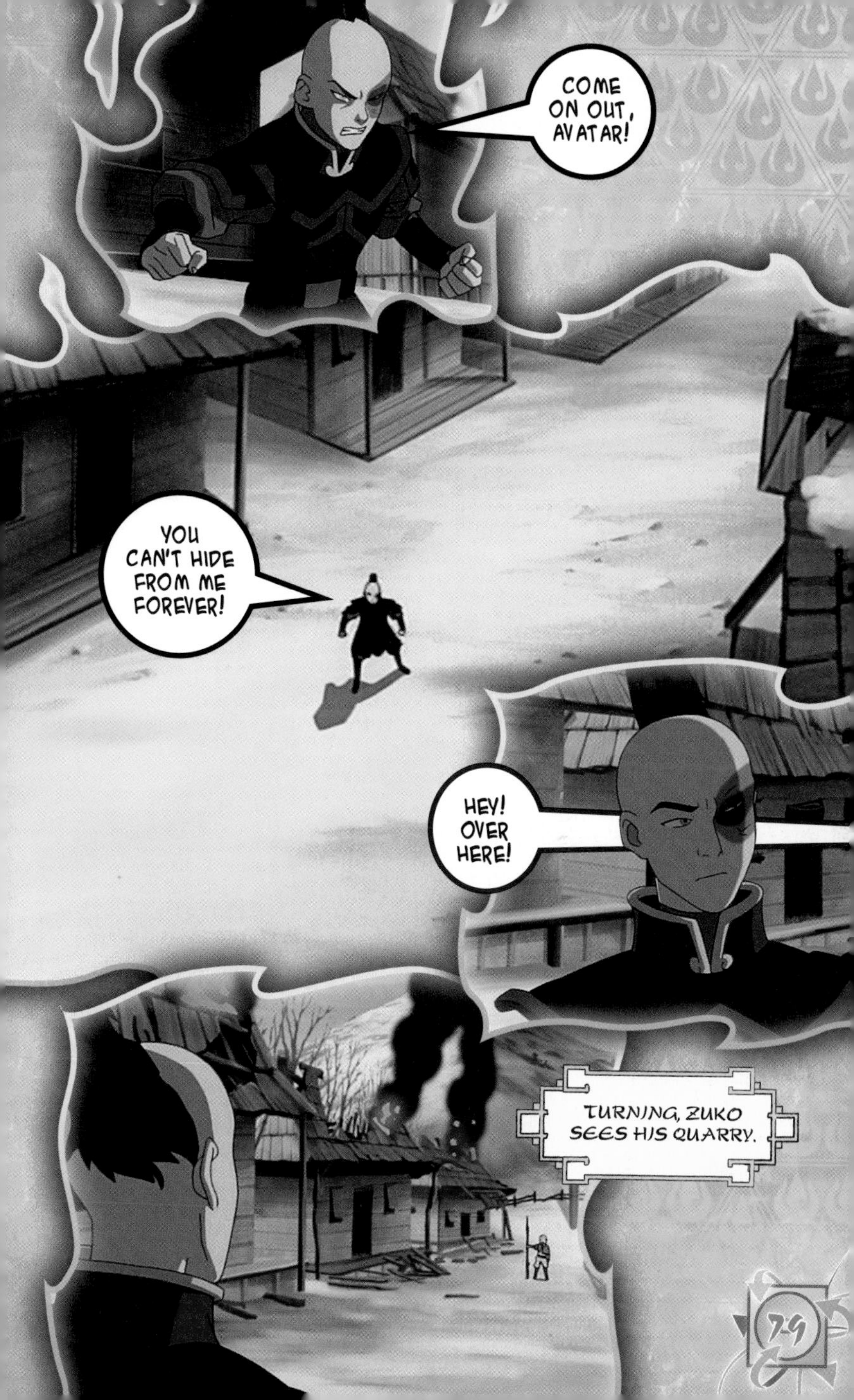

COME ON OUT, AVATAR!
YOU CAN'T HIDE FROM ME FOREVER!
HEY! OVER HERE!
TURNING, ZUKO SEES HIS QUARRY.

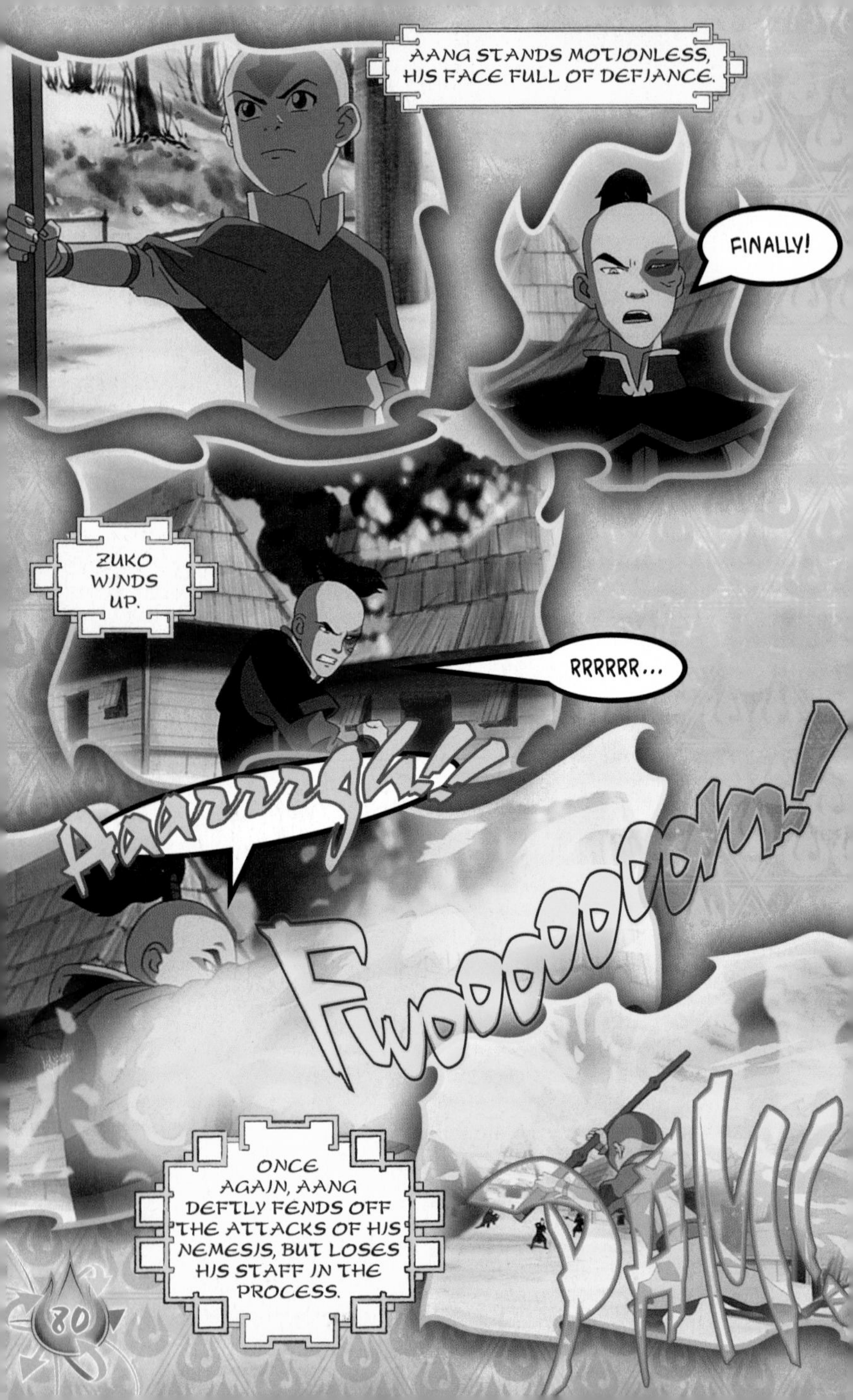
AANG STANDS MOTIONLESS, HIS FACE FULL OF DEFIANCE.
FINALLY!
ZUKO WINDS UP.
RRRRRR...
Aaarrrgh!!
ONCE AGAIN, AANG DEFTLY FENDS OFF THE ATTACKS OF HIS NEMESIS, BUT LOSES HIS STAFF IN THE PROCESS.

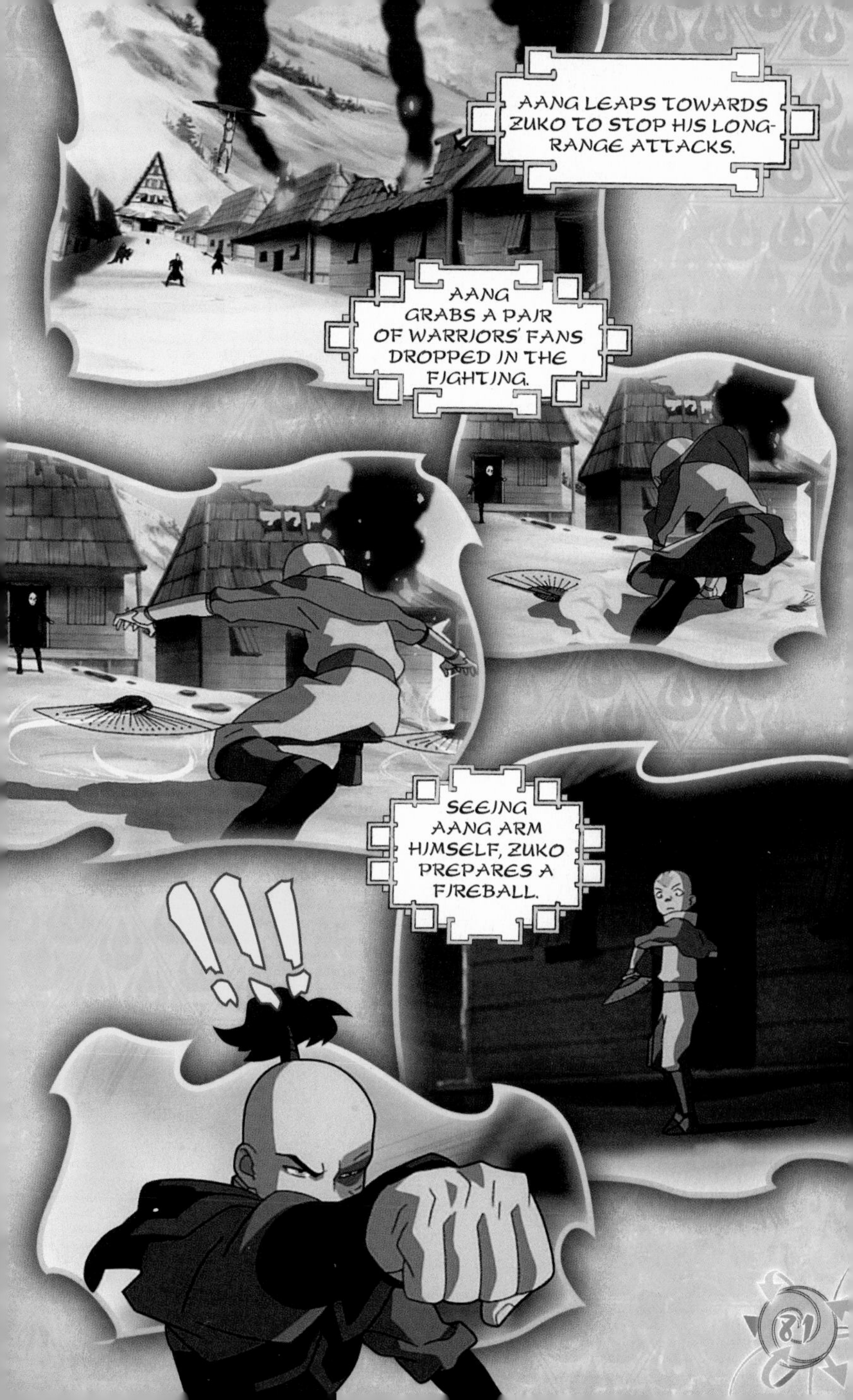
AANG LEAPS TOWARDS ZUKO TO STOP HIS LONG-RANGE ATTACKS.
AANG GRABS A PAIR OF WARRIORS' FANS DROPPED IN THE FIGHTING.
SEEING AANG ARM HIMSELF, ZUKO PREPARES A FIREBALL.
!!!

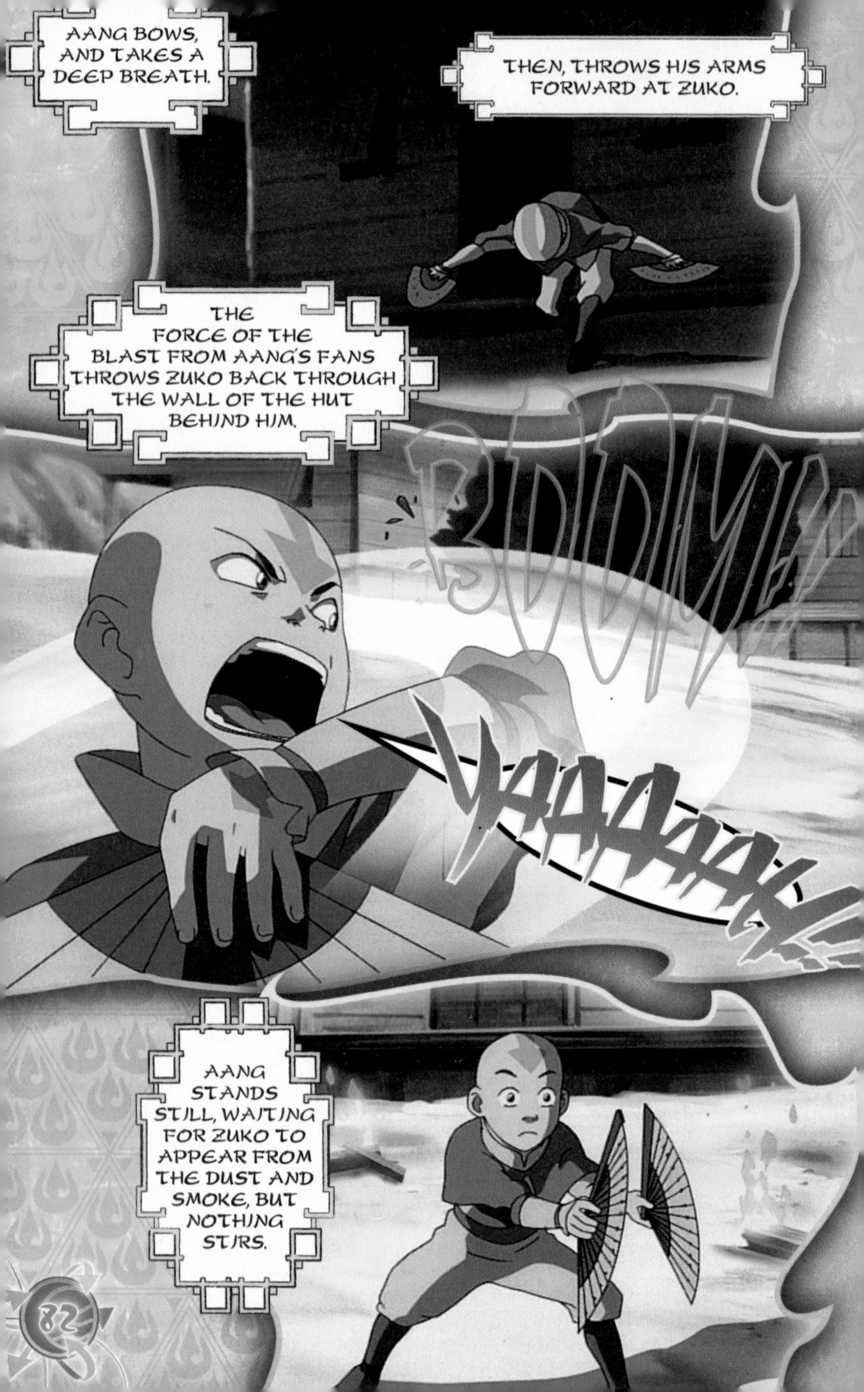
AANG BOWS, AND TAKES A DEEP BREATH.
THEN, THROWS HIS ARMS FORWARD AT ZUKO.
THE FORCE OF THE BLAST FROM AANG'S FANS THROWS ZUKO BACK THROUGH THE WALL OF THE HUT BEHIND HIM.
BOOM!
YAAAAH!
AANG STANDS STILL, WAITING FOR ZUKO TO APPEAR FROM THE DUST AND SMOKE, BUT NOTHING STIRS.

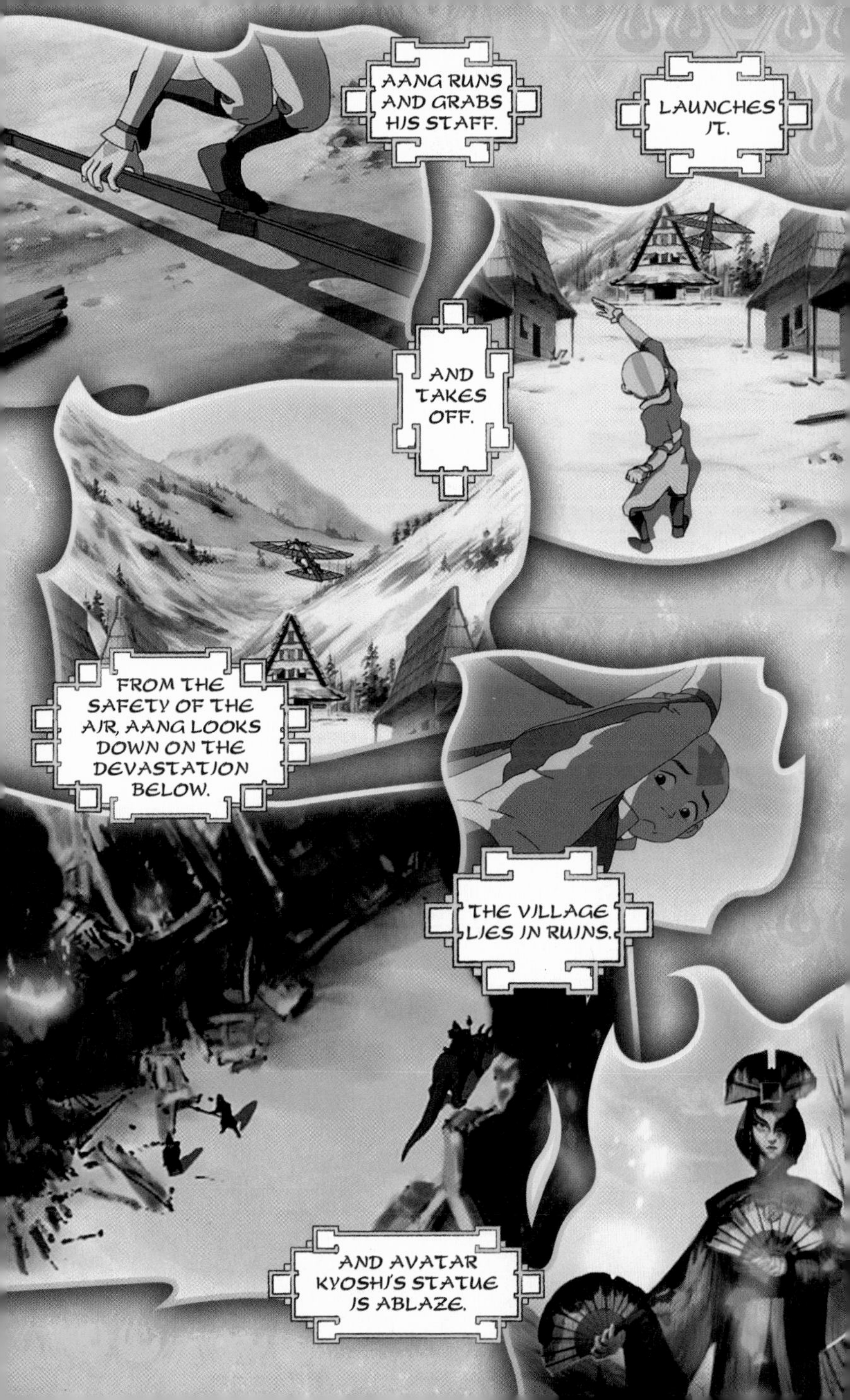
AANG RUNS AND GRABS HIS STAFF.
LAUNCHES IT.
AND TAKES OFF.
FROM THE SAFETY OF THE AIR, AANG LOOKS DOWN ON THE DEVASTATION BELOW.
THE VILLAGE LIES IN RUINS.
AND AVATAR KYOSHI'S STATUE IS ABLAZE.

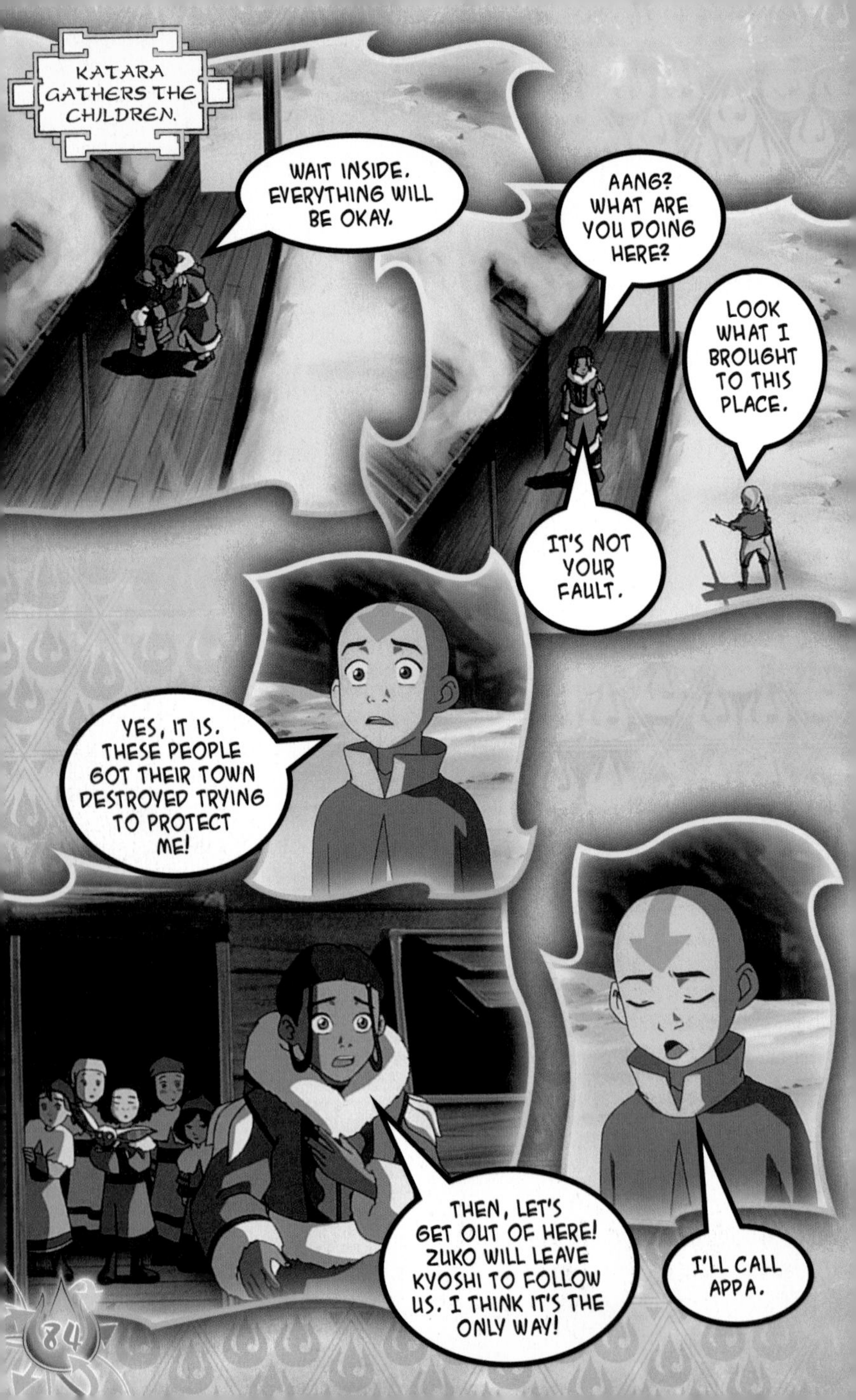
KATARA GATHERS THE CHILDREN.
WAIT INSIDE. EVERYTHING WILL BE OKAY.
AANG? WHAT ARE YOU DOING HERE?
LOOK WHAT I BROUGHT TO THIS PLACE.
IT'S NOT YOUR FAULT.
YES, IT IS. THESE PEOPLE GOT THEIR TOWN DESTROYED TRYING TO PROTECT ME!
THEN, LET'S GET OUT OF HERE! ZUKO WILL LEAVE KYOSHI TO FOLLOW US. I THINK IT'S THE ONLY WAY!
I'LL CALL APPA.

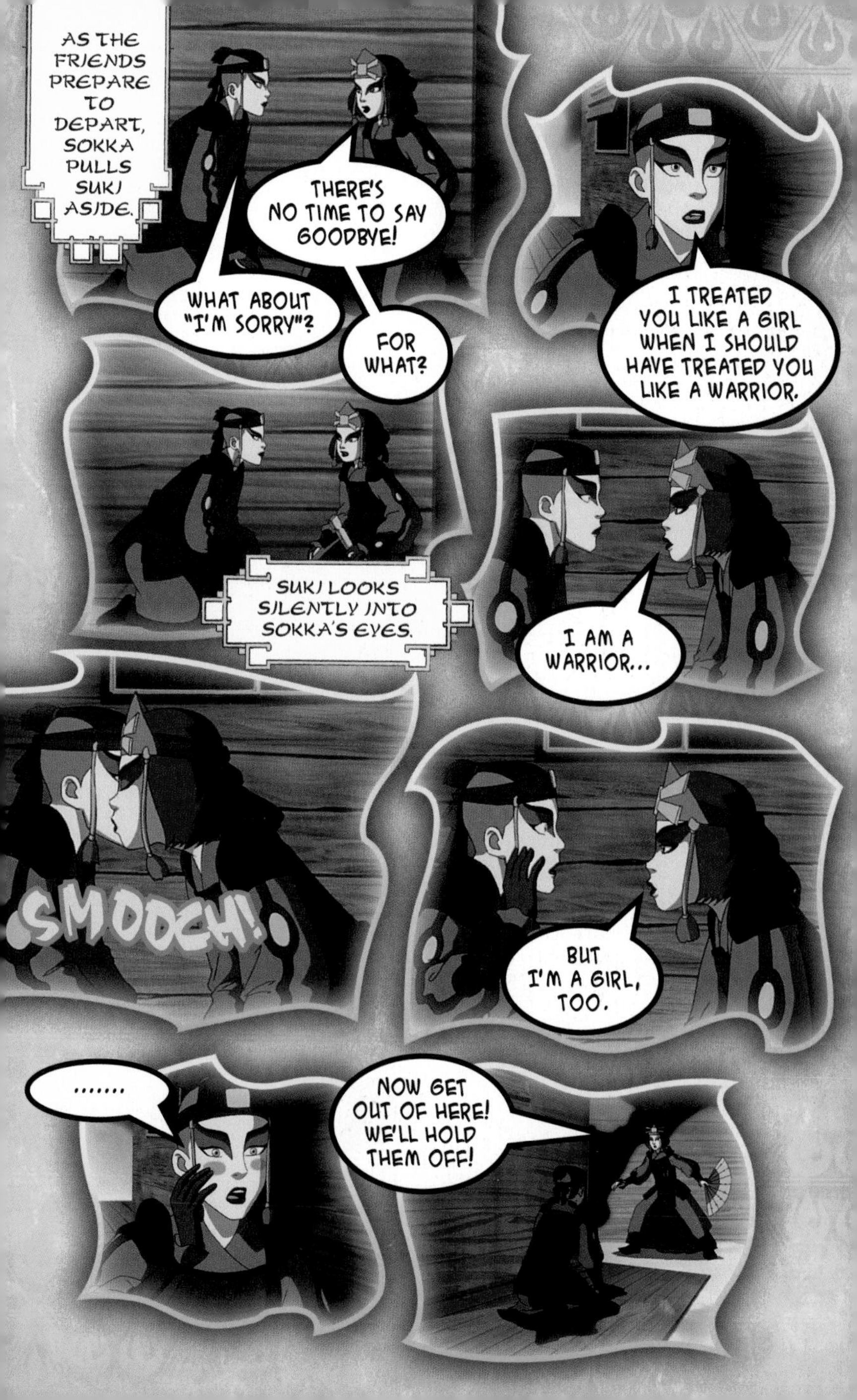
AS THE FRIENDS PREPARE TO DEPART, SOKKA PULLS SUKI ASIDE.
THERE'S NO TIME TO SAY GOODBYE!
WHAT ABOUT "I'M SORRY"?
FOR WHAT?
I TREATED YOU LIKE A GIRL WHEN I SHOULD HAVE TREATED YOU LIKE A WARRIOR.
SUKI LOOKS SILENTLY INTO SOKKA'S EYES.
I AM A WARRIOR...
BUT I'M A GIRL, TOO.
SMOOCH!
....
NOW GET OUT OF HERE! WE'LL HOLD THEM OFF!

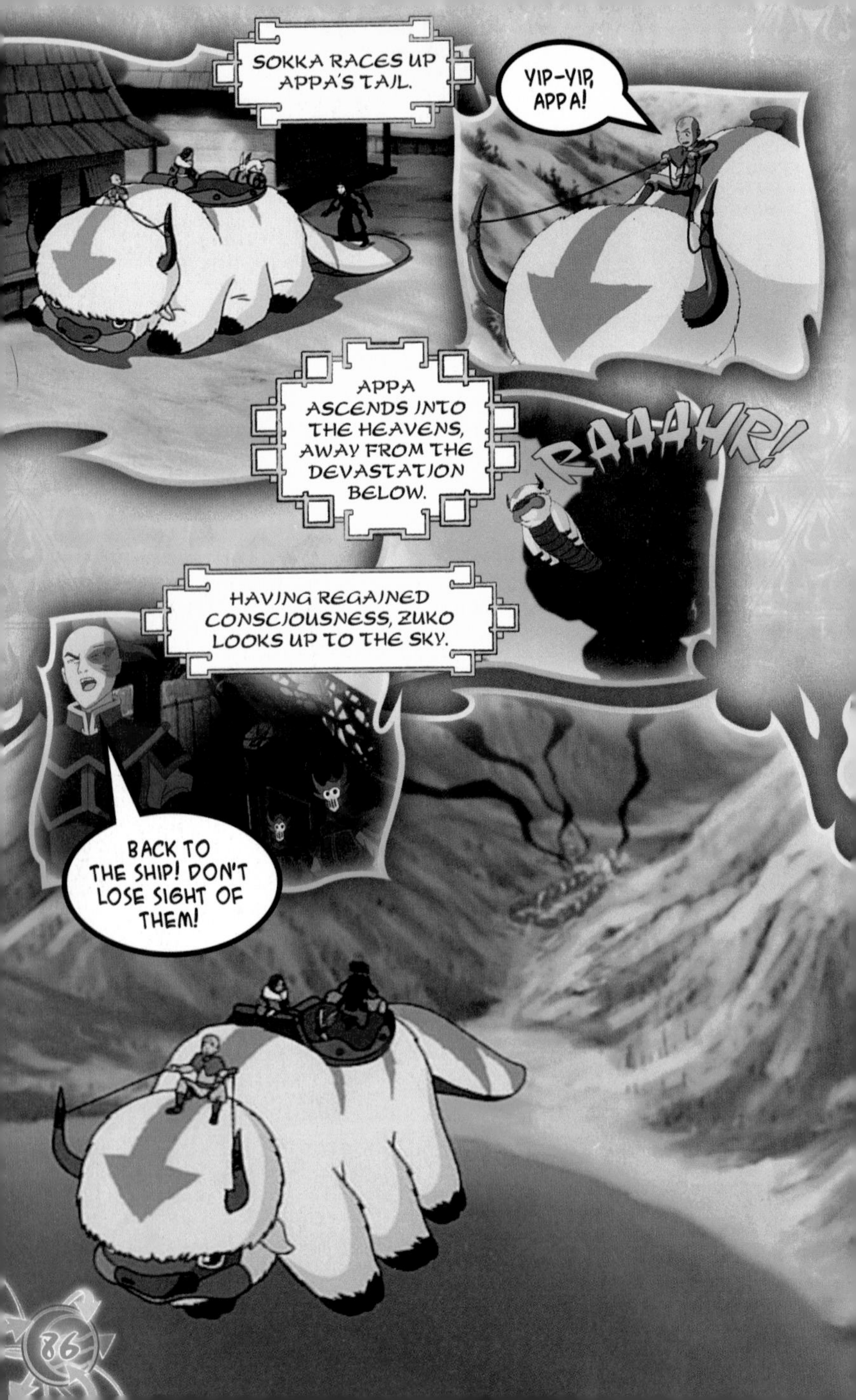
SOKKA RACES UP APPA'S TAIL.
YIP-YIP, APPA!
APPA ASCENDS INTO THE HEAVENS, AWAY FROM THE DEVASTATION BELOW.
RAAAAHR!
HAVING REGAINED CONSCIOUSNESS, ZUKO LOOKS UP TO THE SKY.
BACK TO THE SHIP! DON'T LOSE SIGHT OF THEM!

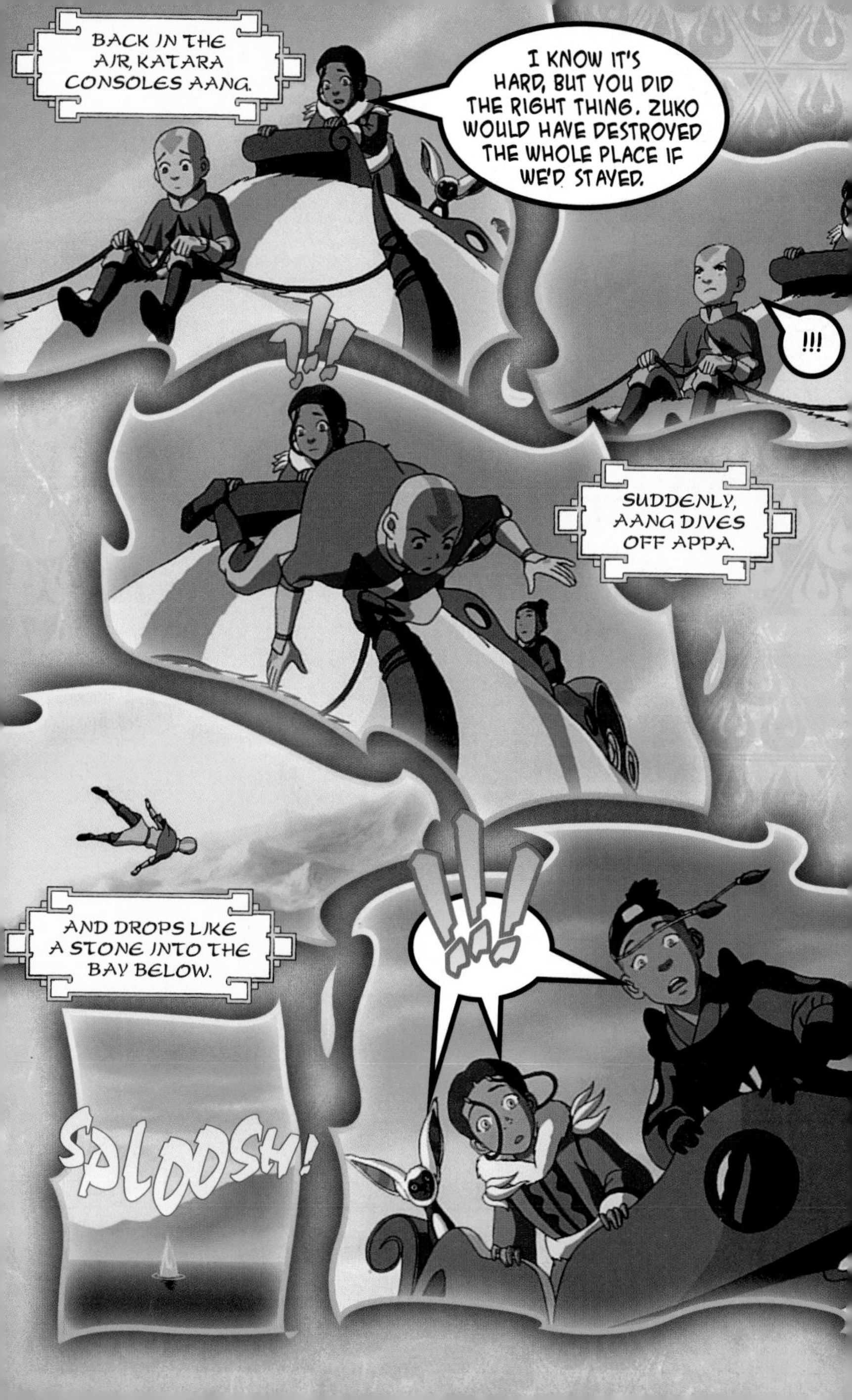
BACK IN THE AIR, KATARA CONSOLES AANG.
I KNOW IT'S HARD, BUT YOU DID THE RIGHT THING. ZUKO WOULD HAVE DESTROYED THE WHOLE PLACE IF WE'D STAYED.
!!!
SUDDENLY, AANG DIVES OFF APPA.
AND DROPS LIKE A STONE INTO THE BAY BELOW.
SPLOOSH!

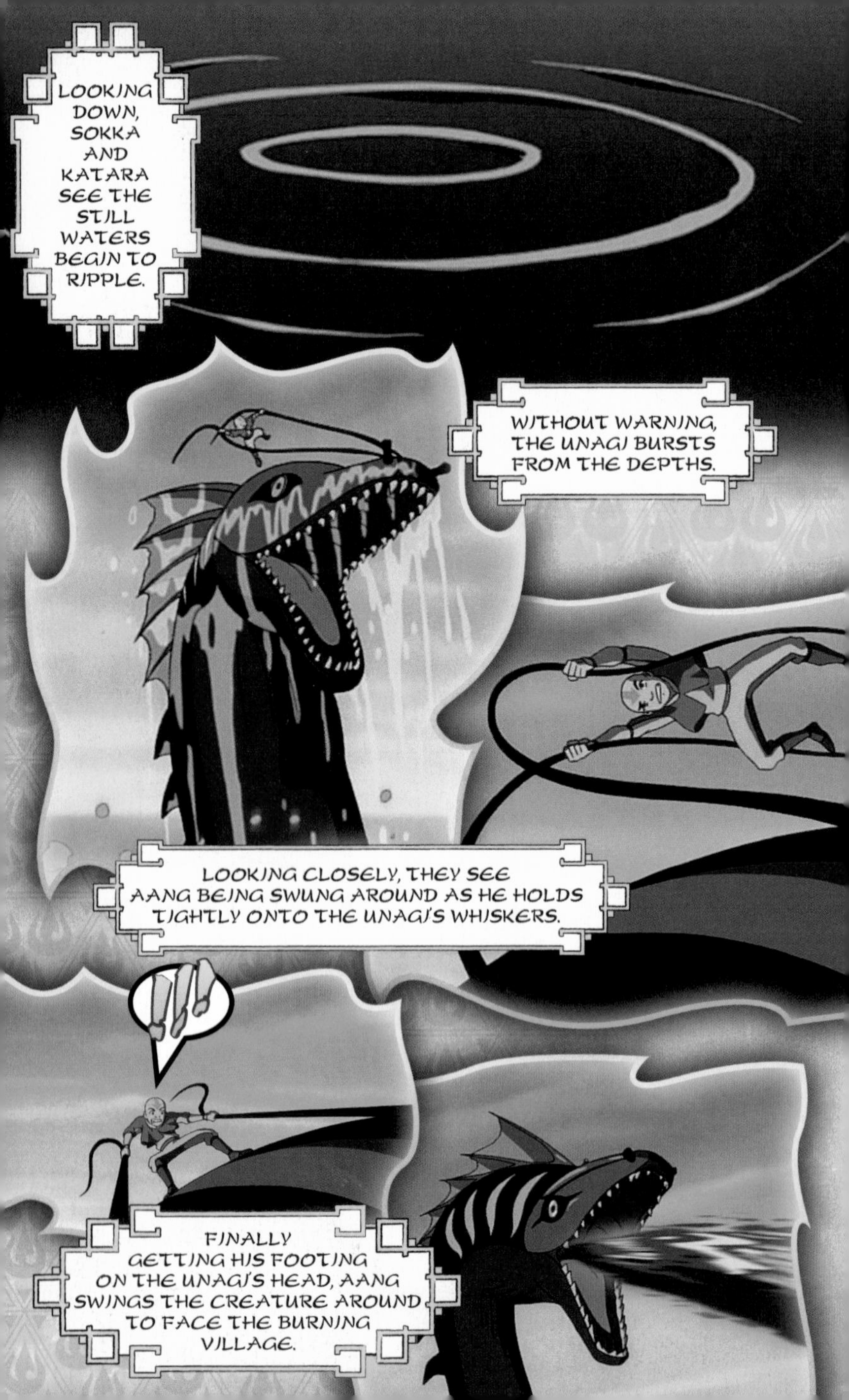
LOOKING DOWN, SOKKA AND KATARA SEE THE STILL WATERS BEGIN TO RIPPLE.
WITHOUT WARNING, THE UNAGI BURSTS FROM THE DEPTHS.
LOOKING CLOSELY, THEY SEE AANG BEING SWUNG AROUND AS HE HOLDS TIGHTLY ONTO THE UNAGI'S WHISKERS.
!!!
FINALLY GETTING HIS FOOTING ON THE UNAGI'S HEAD, AANG SWINGS THE CREATURE AROUND TO FACE THE BURNING VILLAGE.

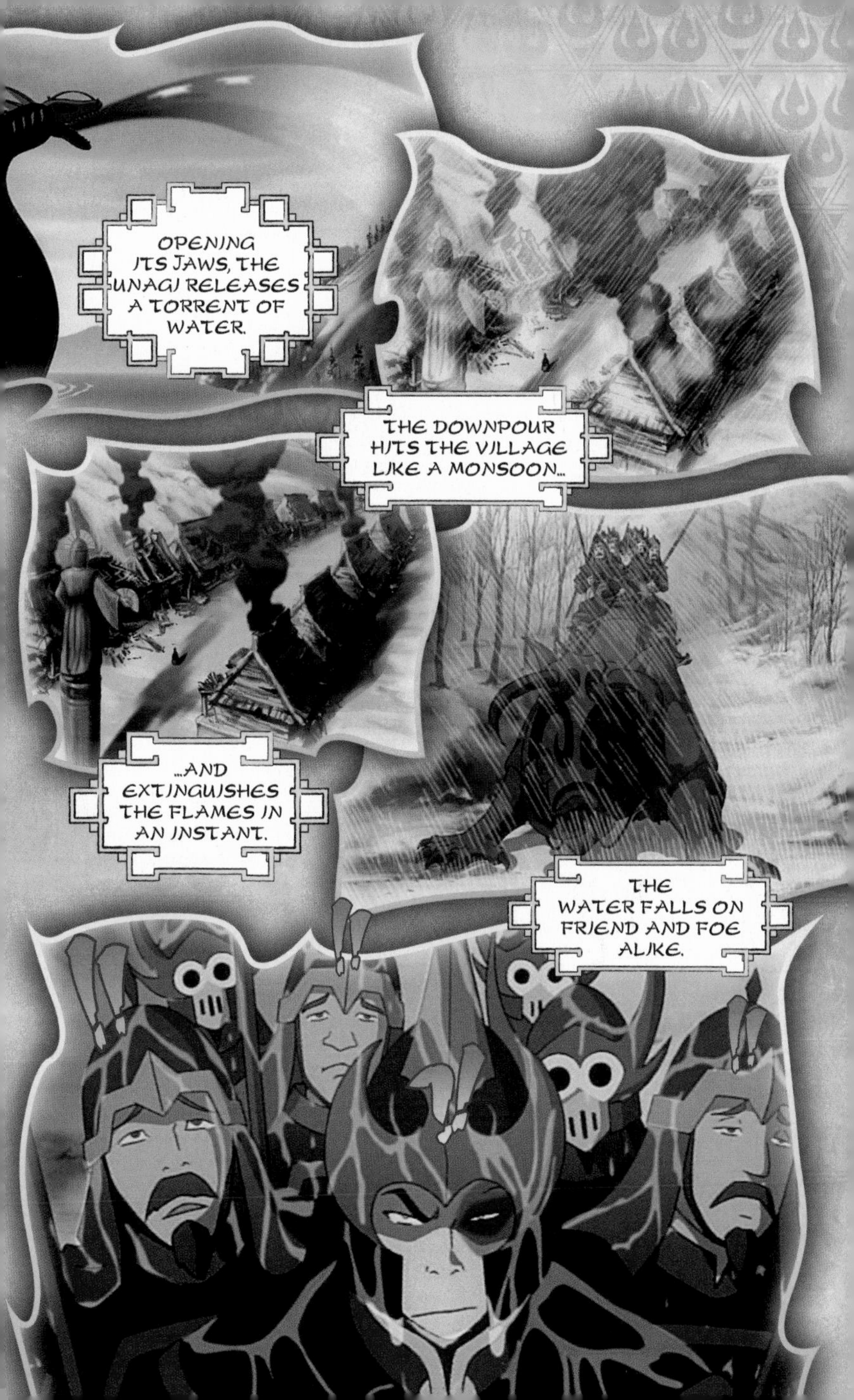
OPENING ITS JAWS, THE UNAGI RELEASES A TORRENT OF WATER.
THE DOWNPOUR HITS THE VILLAGE LIKE A MONSOON...
...AND EXTINGUISHES THE FLAMES IN AN INSTANT.
THE WATER FALLS ON FRIEND AND FOE ALIKE.

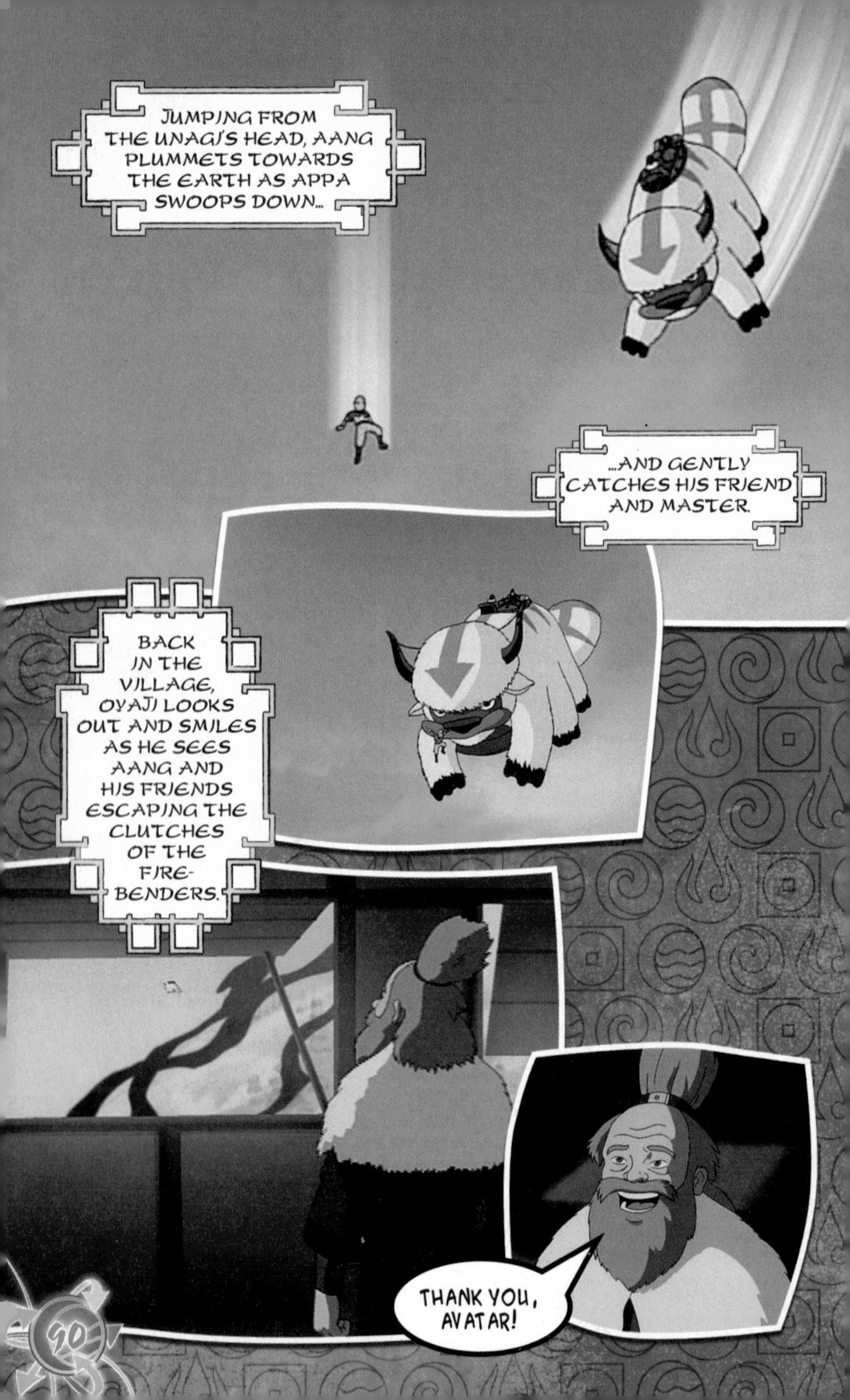
JUMPING FROM THE UNAGI'S HEAD, AANG PLUMMETS TOWARDS THE EARTH AS APPA SWOOPS DOWN...
...AND GENTLY CATCHES HIS FRIEND AND MASTER.
BACK IN THE VILLAGE, OYAJI LOOKS OUT AND SMILES AS HE SEES AANG AND HIS FRIENDS ESCAPING THE CLUTCHES OF THE FIRE-BENDERS.
THANK YOU, AVATAR!

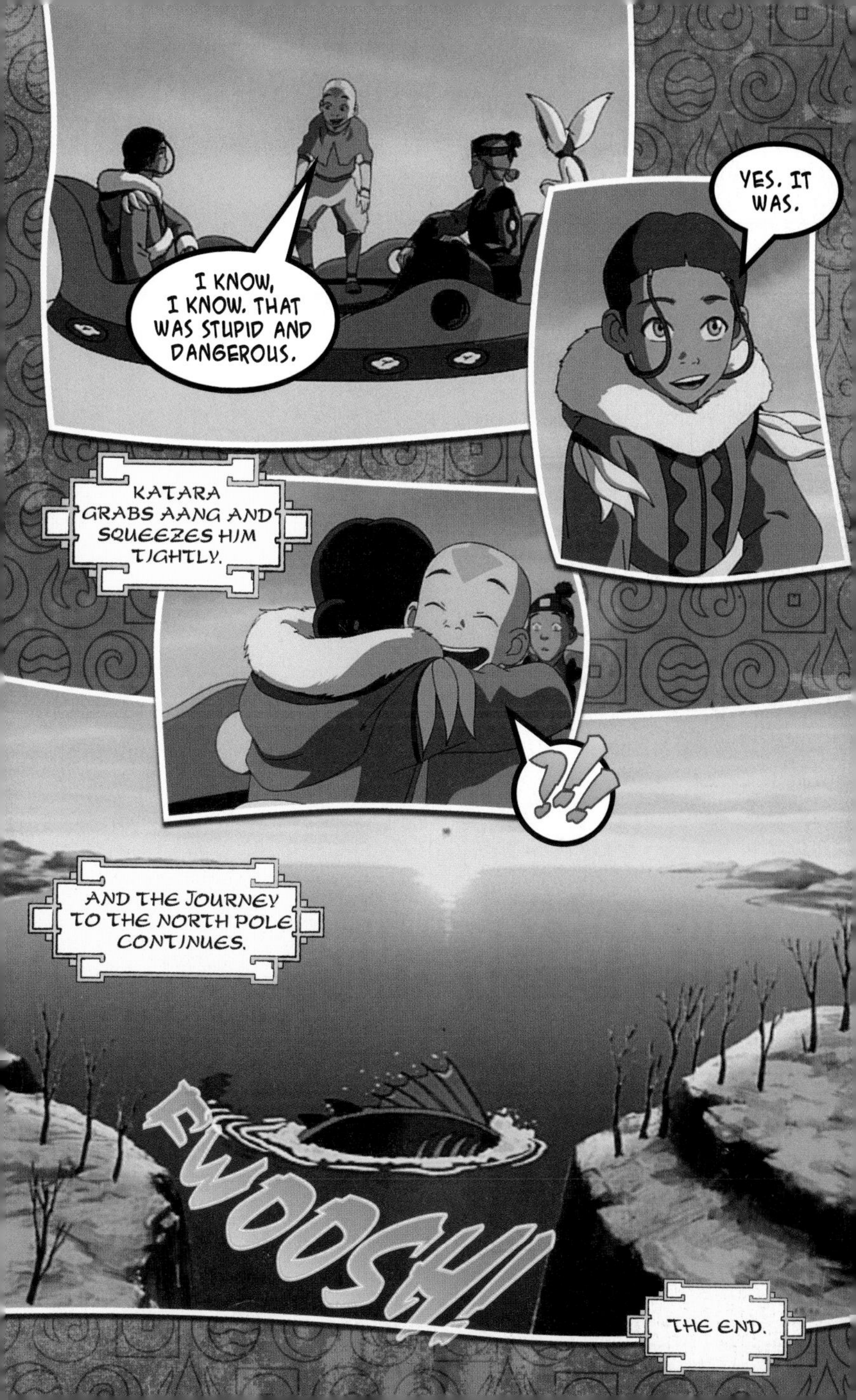
I KNOW, I KNOW. THAT WAS STUPID AND DANGEROUS.
YES. IT WAS.
KATARA GRABS AANG AND SQUEEZES HIM TIGHTLY.
!!
AND THE JOURNEY TO THE NORTH POLE CONTINUES.
FWOOSH!
THE END.

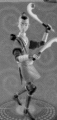

- Aladdin
- All Grown Up
- The Amanda Show
- Avatar
- Bambi
- Barbie™ as the Princess and the Pauper
- Barbie™ Fairytopia
- Barbie™ of Swan Lake
- Chicken Little
- Cinderella
- Drake & Josh
- Duel Masters
- The Fairly OddParents
- Finding Nemo
- Future Greatest Stars of the NBA:
  LeBron James, Dwyane Wade
  and Carmelo Anthony

- G.I. Joe Spy Troops
- Greatest Stars of the NBA: Tim Duncan
- Greatest Stars of the NBA: Kevin Garnett
- Greatest Stars of the NBA: Allen Iverson
- Greatest Stars of the NBA: Jason Kidd
- Greatest Stars of the NBA: Shaquille O'Neal
- The Incredibles
- The Adventures of Jimmy Neutron: Boy Genius
- Kim Possible
- Lilo & Stitch: The Series
- Lizzie McGuire
- Madagascar
- Mucha Lucha!
- Pooh's Heffalump Movie
- Power Rangers
- The Princess Diaries 2
- Rave Master

- Romeo!
- Shrek 2
- SpongeBob SquarePants
- Spy Kids 2
- Spy Kids 3-D: Game Over
- That's So Raven
- Totally Spies
- Transformers

COLLECT THEM ALL!

Now available
wherever books are sold or at
www.TOKYOPOP.com/shop

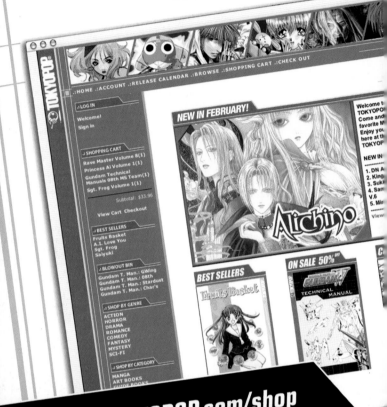